Elite • 102

Santa Anna's Mexican Army 1821–48

René Chartrand • Illustrated by Bill Younghusband

First published in Great Britain in 2004 by Osprey Publishing
Elms Court, Chapel Way, Botley, Oxford OX2 9LP, United Kingdom
Email: info@ospreypublishing.com

ISBN 1 84176 667 4

Editor: Martin Windrow
Design: Alan Hamp
Index by Glyn Sutcliffe
Originated by The Electronic Page Company, Cwmbran, UK
Printed in China through World Print Ltd.

FOR A CATALOGUE OF ALL BOOKS PUBLISHED BY
OSPREY MILITARY AND AVIATION PLEASE CONTACT:

The Marketing Manager, Osprey Direct UK
PO Box 140, Wellingborough, Northants, NN8 2FA, United Kingdom
Email: info@ospreydirect.co.uk

The Marketing Manager, Osprey Direct USA
c/o MBI Publishing, 729 Prospect Avenue, Osceola, WI 54020, USA
Email: info@ospreydirectusa.com

www.ospreypublishing.com

Dedication

To the memory of the late Detmar Finke, friend, colleague, and pioneer researcher of Mexican military material culture.

Acknowledgements

Mrs Carol Haarmann of Washington, DC; James L.Kochan of Harpers Ferry, WV; Gen Hector Lopez Ortega, former Military Attaché at the Embassy of Mexico in Canada; Kevin R.Young in Texas; the Anne S.K.Brown Military Collection at Brown University, Providence, RI, USA; the Public Records Office at Kew, UK; and the National Library of Canada in Ottawa.

Author's Note

The cut of the Mexican uniforms reconstructed in the color plates generally follows that of the French Army regulations of the 1820s to 1840s, since these were the main inspiration for the dress of Mexican armies. However, there were obviously many local variations as shown by artwork or surviving items, such as shorter coat tails, an apparent lack of shoulder straps, a variety of shako plates, and the wearing of sandals.

With regards to the hues of colors described in this text, blue was meant to be a dark blue and green was also dark. However, artwork occasionally shows somewhat lighter hues of blue and green because of the varying qualities of uniform cloth. Officers had better quality materials and therefore dark blue and dark green uniforms. Crimson on Mexican uniforms was a much brighter color than American or British crimson, often passing for red. Scarlet or red ranged from the 'brick red' of the common soldiers to a fine scarlet for officers. White, especially for waistcoats and breeches, could also assume a creamy color. Gray ranged from a light blue-gray to a dark hue.

Artist's Note

Readers may care to note that the original paintings from which the color plates in this book were prepared are available for private sale. All reproduction copyright whatsoever is retained by the Publishers. All enquiries should be addressed to:

Bill Younghusband
'Moorfield', Kilcolman West, Buttevant, County Cork, Eire

The Publishers regret that they can enter into no correspondence upon this matter.

SANTA ANNA'S MEXICAN ARMY 1821–48

INTRODUCTION

General de Division Antonio Lopez de Santa Anna, c1830, wearing the 1823 dress uniform in this painting by Charles Paris. The red lapels and collar are piped in blue, the cuffs in scarlet; added touches are blue epaulette loops embroidered in gold, and blue cuff flaps piped in scarlet. In Texas he was described as 'a man of medium size, dressed in a dark blue coat, light blue vest [obviously the sash], with red trimmings [lapels] upon the breast, gold buttons and a gold epaulette on each shoulder.' Santa Anna was President of Mexico on 11 different occasions between 1833 and 1855. (Museo de la Ciudad de Mexico; author's photo)

ANTONIO LOPEZ DE SANTA ANNA (1794–1876), a general in 1821 and president of Mexico eleven times between 1833 and 1855, dominated his country's turbulent political life for some 35 years. A man of great charm, energy and political ability, and obviously gifted with a strong charisma, he was also a vain, unprincipled and remorseless knave who led his country to disaster.

As a soldier, he was brave enough, and had the ability to prevail against local revolts. He was successful against the largely ineffective Spanish at Tampico in 1829; but it was another matter when he faced Texans in 1836, the French in 1838 and the United States in 1846–47. His army had many problems, as will be seen in this book, possibly the worst being that it never had senior officers who carried out state-of-the-art military planning rather than concocting political coups. The result was that what had started out as a fairly decent, well equipped army in the 1820s was outclassed by the 1840s. Yet in the final struggle, the army that Santa Anna led was noted for its brave and stubborn fighting and some heroic stands to rival the finest feats in military annals. The tragedy was that Mexican soldiers did not have leaders worthy of their outstanding valor.

Much of this book is devoted to the Mexican soldier's material culture, his uniforms and arms in particular. Santa Anna loved uniforms, and decreed some very colorful dress for his soldiers, especially from the late 1830s. Yet, as we reveal in this overview from records of issues and stores, the Mexican army – particularly in the 1840s – often actually wore uniforms that bore no resemblance to the dress regulations. The arms and accoutrements remained basically of the Napoleonic era right up to the end of the war with the United States in 1848. The few rifles imported in the 1820s appear to have been little used, and there is no trace of significant technological improvements to the armament.[1]

Historical background

From 1810, Mexico was shaken by several large scale insurrections against the Spanish regime. Contrary to other uprisings in Latin America, the Spanish and royalist Mexican forces had beaten the revolutionaries

---

1 The use of rifles in Mexico has been the subject of much confusion through mistranslation of Spanish terms. *Fusil* means musket; *carabina* means rifle. Further confusion arose from Mexican references to American riflemen as *rifleros*, a term also used for such units when they were eventually raised in Mexico. The Spanish term for carbine is *tercerola*. The *escopeta* was a peculiar type of musket, very sturdy, that originated in Catalonia and was used as a hunting and light infantry weapon if long-barreled, or as a cavalry carbine if short. It was especially popular with Mexican Presidial cavalry on the northern frontier.

José Maria Morelos was leader of a major uprising against Spanish authority in 1812. He declared Mexico's independence on September 13, 1813, but was later defeated by the Spanish and executed in December 1815. In this portrait he wears the uniform of a Mexican *generalissimo*, almost identical to that of Spanish generals. (Museo Nacional de Historia, Mexico; author's photo)

by late 1815. After 1815 what was left of the revolutionaries took to the hills and, mostly under the leadership of Vincente Guerrero and Guadalupe Victoria, waged guerrilla warfare with moderate success.

In 1821 a revolution in Spain itself, which was won by liberals, produced an extraordinary effect in Mexico. The Spanish and those Mexicans loyal to the crown were mostly conservatives who now found themselves politically isolated. A Spanish force led by General Augustin de Iturbide entered negotiations with Guerrero; the two drafted the Plan of Iguala, and united their forces to fight for the Three Guarantees: independence from Spain, equal rights for all peninsular or Spanish descendants in Mexico, supremacy of the Catholic Church. Their 'Army of the Three Guarantees' did not meet much opposition; many other 'loyalist' troops rallied to it, and it entered Mexico City in triumph. Mexico became independent from Spain, and Iturbide was proclaimed Emperor Augustin I in late 1821.

With its independence, Mexico entered a period of political instability which lasted for over a century. The first major trauma came as a result of rapid discontent with the imperial regime among the army's generals. Once proclaimed emperor, Iturbide and his friends ransacked the Mexican treasury, the emperor himself pocketing some 120,000 pesos – an enormous sum – and within a year the country was driven into debt. This looting of the nation's wealth provoked a coup d'état led by army generals in March 1823. The Republic was proclaimed, and General Victoria became president in 1824.

The following year the Spanish were finally expelled from their last enclave, the fortress of San Juan de Ulloa in the harbor of Vera Cruz. In 1829, a Spanish army landed in Mexico in a last bid to reconquer its former colony, but General Santa Anna beat the Spanish force at Tampico on September 11. The 1830s and 1840s were marked by repeated military coups and constant internal strife, notably in 1832, 1835, 1839 and 1845. The 1836 war in Texas against its American settlers had very negative consequences. Santa Anna's victories at Goliad and at the famous Alamo battle were marred by his orders that no prisoners be taken; this barbarism brought condemnation by France and Britain, both powers feeling that 'great and lasting disgrace must fall upon the nation under whose flag such atrocities have been committed' (PRO, FO 50/99).

Beaten by the Texans at San Jacinto, the Mexican army retreated south of the Rio Grande, which was claimed as the border by the new Republic of Texas. In December 1838 the French fleet attacked and took Vera Cruz following non-payment of Mexico's debts to France. In 1842 the Mexican army made several forays into Texas, capturing several towns including San Antonio without resistance from the Texans; the

Undress coat of Generalissimo Morelos, c1813–15, returned to Mexico by Spain in 1910 on the centenary of the first Mexican revolution. The coat is all blue, with silver buttons, lace and embroidery; the pockets and skirt pleats are piped scarlet. (Museo Nacional de Historia, Mexico; author's photo)

Mexican statistics, pre–1848

Mexico has 24 states and territories and one Federal District.
Population (1841 census): 7,044,140
Mexico City: c200,000

Currency:
16 silver *pesos* (or dollars) = 1 gold ounce
8 silver *reals* = 1 *peso*
4 copper *cuartillas* = 1 *real*

Prices and wages:
Bread = half *real* for a pound weight
Sugar = 1 *real* per pound
Man's suit (good quality) = 60 *pesos*
Man's pair of shoes = 1 *peso*
Riding horse = 200 *pesos*

President's salary = 3,000 *pesos* per month
General's salary = 500 *pesos*
Colonel's salary = 325 *pesos*
Lieutenant's salary = 39 *pesos*
Soldier's wages = 12 *pesos* (without food)
Servant's wages = 6 *pesos* (with food & board)
Seamstress's wages = 10 *pesos*

Measures:
1 *vara castallena* (Castilian yard, 0.83m, c2ft 9in)
  = 36 *pulgadas*
1 *pie castellano* (Castilian foot, 0.27m, c10.9in)
  = 12 *pulgadas*
1 *pulgada castellana* (Castilian inch)
  = 23.2mm, c0.9in

USA threatened war, but a negotiated peace was finally achieved with the help of France and Britain in 1843. In December 1845, Texas was annexed to the United States.

Relations between Mexico and its northern neighbor went from bad to worse and, on April 23, 1846, Mexico declared war on the United States. The US did not formally reciprocate until May 13, by which time several victories had already been won by General Zachary Taylor's army from Texas. The Mexicans were beaten in the north at Palo Alto and Resaca de La Palma on May 8–9, at Monterey on September 20–24, and at Buena Vista on February 22–23, 1847. The US Navy blockaded the Mexican coast and occupied Tampico, landing an army under General Winfield Scott which took Vera Cruz on March 25. The Americans then marched on Mexico City, defeating the Mexicans at Cerro Gordo in April, at Contreras and Churubusco in August, and at Molino del Rey, Chapultepec and Puebla in September. On the 14th of that month Scott's army marched into Mexico City.

Apart from sporadic minor engagements and guerrilla raids, resistance collapsed, and peace was concluded on February 2, 1848. By this treaty of Guadalupe Hidalgo, the vast but sparsely populated northern territories from New Mexico to Alta California, previously occupied by the Americans, were ceded to the United States.

ORGANIZATION OF THE ARMY

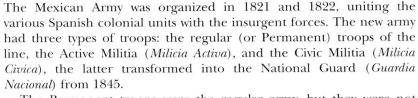

The Mexican Army was organized in 1821 and 1822, uniting the various Spanish colonial units with the insurgent forces. The new army had three types of troops: the regular (or Permanent) troops of the line, the Active Militia (*Milicia Activa*), and the Civic Militia (*Milicia Civica*), the latter transformed into the National Guard (*Guardia Nacional*) from 1845.

The Permanent troops were the regular army, but they were not alone in performing active duty in peacetime. There were also a number of units belonging to the *Milicia Activa* – the active duty militia. This organization, inherited from the Provincial units of the Spanish regime, consisted of corps that were partly or wholly embodied on active duty – which, in Mexico, would last many years.

The *Milicia Civica*, organized from 1822, was the basic reserve into which, by law, any Mexican male between the ages of 18 and 40 years and able to bear arms could be enlisted. This was a true national militia; although they would occasionally drill, they were to be called up only for local police duties or in emergencies. The units were to be made up of volunteers or, failing that, by compulsory listing of one man in every hundred.

From September 10, 1823, the army came under 17 General Commandancies (*Commandancias Generales*) and seven smaller Particular Commandancies (*Commandancias Particulares*). During 1839, the army was reorganized into six divisions covering the various states. The 1st Division had its HQ at Toluca and included Mexico, Queretaro and Michoacan (reorganized into the Reserve Army in 1845); the 2nd Division's HQ was at Jalapa and comprised Puebla, Vera Cruz, Tabasco and Oaxaca; the 3rd Division was headquartered at Lagos and covered Jalisco, Zacatecas, Aguascaliente, Guanajuato and San Luis Potosi. The 4th Division (also called the Army of the North) comprised Nuevo Leon, Coahuila and Tamaulipas; the 5th included Chihuahua, Durango and Nuevo Mexico; and the 6th consisted of Sonora and Sinaloa – the HQs of the last three divisions could vary as needed.

There were also four General Commandancies: Mexico City, Yucatan, Chiapas and the Californias. The towns of Vera Cruz and Campeche and the forts of San Juan de Ulloa, Perote and Acapulco each had a military governor-commandant. All senior posts were filled by generals except for the general-commandants of Yucatan and the Californias, who were colonels. Another 17 cities had military commandants, either generals or colonels. Each division and command had its army auditors,

General of Division Guadalupe Victoria in his 1823 regulation uniform, complete with white piping edging the red facings. The broad sword belt is embroidered with gold and has a large, rectangular gilt plate; the sword has a gilt guard and ivory grip. Gen Victoria was President of Mexico 1824–29 – the only president before the late 1860s who managed to serve his full term. (Museo Nacional de Historia, Mexico; author's photo)

treasurers and clerks, as well as junior generals and staff officers. Some were also to be found in the commandancies, towns and forts, so that there was usually a flurry of gold lace and feathers in any headquarters.

In 1825 British and French diplomats estimated the actual strength of the army at 30,000 ill armed and badly clothed men. That year, Minister of War Gomez Pedraza wanted to augment the forces to 67,700 men and, thanks to loans from British banks, purchased 90,000 muskets, 14,000 carbines, 2,000 rifles, 20,000 swords, 5,000 pairs of pistols and 20,000 uniforms from Britain. The rifles were issued to some light companies, although to what extent remains unclear.[2]

Additional cloth and linen uniforms were procured in the country. The army 'improved wonderfully, both in appearance and discipline; and that as much has been done, as the time would admit of, towards recreating an Esprit de Corps' (PRO, FO 50/31). This was not to last for long. In spite of a contract for 20,000 uniforms in 1832, the army was often badly clothed by the time of the Texas war. Some 20,000 muskets, 3,000 carbines, 3,000 cavalry sabers and 6,000 infantry sabers were ordered in 1842 and 1844, as well as 'very brilliant' new uniforms.[3]

In May 1846 the Mexican army had 24,550 men, but this was not enough; on August 28 the government announced that 'All Mexicans from the age of fifteen to sixty' could be drafted, and deserters were pardoned if they rejoined the army. Nevertheless, although many National Guards mobilized, Santa Anna could only muster 20,000–25,000 men at most for his main army.

Enlisted men were usually levied by force amongst poor Indian peasants who, once in the army, were 'tattered, ill fed, kicked, and buffeted about by drunken and sober officers', who were also prone to embezzling the pay which should have reached them. Naturally, they often deserted, and might indulge in looting – at first merely to feed themselves, but such practices, once begun, tend to spiral. However, the Mexican peasant was a very tough soldier, and if given the opportunity would put up a very hard fight. The army's main weakness lay in its officer corps. The generals were more concerned with political maneuvers and self-enrichment than with the art of war. The regimental officers were observed as being brave enough, but largely deficient in military education and training. Few units could avoid the contagion of Mexico's tumultuous politics, and would be at times loyal to the government, and at times swept up in mutinies, depending upon

General of Division Vincente Guerrero, c1829, wearing the 1823 dress uniform for generals but with the facings edged with blue rather than white piping. The size of the epaulettes has been exaggerated by the artist. Guerrero was president from April to December 1829. During his short tenure his government abolished slavery, which had only been allowed in Texas since 1810 – a decision which enraged most Texans and soured their relations with the Mexican government. (Museo Nacional de Historia, Mexico; author's photo)

2 These shipments arrived in early 1826 (FO 50/28), not in 1824 as given in *El Ejercito Mexicano* (Mexico, 1979). In all there were 111,564 muskets, 15,280 carbines, 2,000 rifles, 8,000 prs pistols, 26,500 sabers and 5,792 lances in 1827.
3 The 1842 and 1844 contracts specified 15,000 muskets from Britain, but the 3,000 cavalry and 6,000 infantry sabers may have been from France, as per *Memoria del secretario… de Guerra marina…* (Mexico, 1845). Lady Frances Calderon de La Barca (*Life in Mexico*) mentioned on October 12, 1842, that 'money had been given to troops in the palace, with orders to purchase new uniforms, which is said to be very brilliant.' These would have been given to troops supporting Santa Anna, on his return to power as president for the sixth time.

the excitement of the day and the allegiance of their officers. Despite the profound damage to the army's cohesion inflicted by decades of civil wars, it is remarkable that many of its elements fought with the heroism of elite troops when confronting a foreign invader.[4]

GENERAL & STAFF OFFICERS

Uniforms

The genesis of Mexican general officers' uniforms can be traced back to the first major uprising in 1810. It appears that one of the first things Father Miguel Hidalgo and his fellow revolutionary leaders did, once their movement was under way, was to design uniforms for themselves. As *Generalissimo*, Hidalgo had a blue coat with scarlet collar, lapels and cuffs, gold and silver embroidery edging the collar, the lapels and the pockets. There were no epaulettes. Revolutionary Captain-General Allende had a similar coat, but with silver lace edging all seams and one row of lace around the cuffs. Insurgent lieutenant-generals had the same with an aiguillette at the right shoulder, and at the left shoulder for *mariscal de campo* – roughly, major-general. Brigadiers had three laces on the cuffs, with a row of embroidery and narrow lace edging the facings.

After Hidalgo's defeat, capture and execution in July 1811, the standard of revolt passed to another cleric, Father José Maria Morelos y Pavon. He too assumed a splendid general's uniform, also blue with scarlet facings edged with gold embroidered lace – one row for the collar and lapels, and three rows on the cuffs. The sash was scarlet with gold embroidery; the breeches were blue with wide gold lace bands;

---

4 The forced levy (*leva*) recruiting system, a sort of legal kidnapping of poor peasants, is described in many sources. The quotation is according to J.M.L.Mora in 1836. Gen Miguel A.Sanchez Lamego, *El Batallon de San Blas 1825–1855* (Mexico, 1964) is a brief chronicle of an heroic outfit, and recounts the political adventures that were typical of the lot of all Mexican units.

and the bicorn hat was laced with gold and bore a white and sky-blue cockade. The other revolutionary generals probably had the same but with only one or two rows of gold embroidered lace on the cuffs. After much campaigning, General Felix Calleja and his Spanish troops managed to crush this revolt in 1815.

The inspiration for these first Mexican generals' uniforms was, unsurprisingly, that of Spanish generals – the only model for such dress that the vast majority of Mexicans had ever seen – and in later years Mexican generals' uniforms would continue to resemble those of the former colonial power. At the time of independence in 1821, these uniforms were Spanish-made or Spanish-inspired, with the addition of red, white and green Mexican cockades, plumes and other insignia. That October the general's uniform was decreed to be a blue coat with scarlet collar, cuffs, lapels and turn-backs, white waistcoat and breeches, white silk stockings with shoes in gala dress or boots in formal duty dress.

A brigadier-general had one row of silver embroidery edging the collar and lapels and one row on the cuffs; buttons of gold or silver stamped with an imperial crown according to the arm of service (i.e. gold for infantry, silver for cavalry); gold or silver epaulettes with an eagle of contrasting color on the strap; a green silk sash with a row of gold or silver embroidery and gold tassels. A brigadier-general who was also colonel of a regiment could wear the regimental uniform with a row of embroidery at the cuffs denoting his rank (this was a common practice in the Spanish army).

A major-general (*mariscal de campo*) had the same except that the embroidery, epaulettes and buttons were of gold, as was the embroidery on the green silk sash. A lieutenant-general had the same as a major-general, but the seams of the coat were also decorated with gold embroidery and the cuffs and sash had two rows of embroidered lace. A captain-general had three rows of gold embroidered lace. A portrait of Iturbide in c1822 shows him with the facings of his coat edged with white piping, the cuffs having three rows of embroidery; his sky-blue silk waist sash has three rows of gold embroidery, and he wears a green, white and red shoulder sash denoting his position of head of state. The dress uniform of other generals was just as superb. British tourist W.Bullock, in Vera Cruz in February 1823, described the 'Republican generals, St [Santa] Anna and Vittoria [Guadalupe Victoria]; they were on horseback, in splendid military costume, and well mounted.' The undress was a plain blue single-breasted coat with gold embroidery on the collar and cuffs. Either white or dark trousers could be worn.

After the fall of the short-lived Empire, uniform regulations for generals of the Mexican Republic were decreed on **October 16, 1823**. They somewhat simplified the dress while confirming most existing items. The dress uniform consisted of a blue coat with scarlet collar, lapels and cuffs, white piping and white (rather than red) turn-backs and gold buttons; a row of gold embroidery of intertwined laurels, palms, and olives edged the collar, lapels, pocket flaps and coat tails. The gold epaulettes, which tended to be very large, each bore a silver Mexican eagle. The brigadier-general had one row of gold embroidery on the cuffs, the general of division had two rows. A silk sash with gold tassels and fringes was worn around the waist, in dark green for brigadier-generals and sky-blue for generals of division. The breeches or pantaloons were white, the boots black; the hat was laced with gold, edged with white plumage and with red, white and green feathers rising from above the tricolor cockade. It seems appropriate to mention here that a French Navy officer was once asked by Gen Santa Anna, the self-proclaimed 'Napoleon of the West,' how the real Napoleon had worn his hat...[5]

The undress uniform consisted, in theory, of a blue coat without lapels or piping. Although not specified in 1823, the collar and cuffs were edged with gold embroidered lace and were often scarlet. Other items were as in the dress uniform.

The regulation of **August 10, 1831** concerning generals' uniforms basically repeated the 1823 decree, but changed the colors of the piping and turn-backs on the dress coat from white to scarlet; the pockets were now specified to be horizontal with three buttons. Gray or blue pantaloons could be worn on all occasions except for gala dress, which still required white. The **August 31, 1840** regulations confirmed the 1831 uniform dress coat, sash and hat, but with eagle ornaments on the turn-backs, and trousers with an inch-wide gold lace (illustrated by G.A.Embleton in MAA 56, *The Mexican-American War 1846–48*). The undress coat was now completely blue with rows of gold rank embroidery on the collar and cuffs; it was to be worn with plain blue trousers, a hat without plumes, and the regulation sash. A blue frock coat could also be worn with the sash. The option for brigadier-generals to wear a regimental uniform with rows of general's embroidery continued. This may have been the case of Gen Mejia, seen at Matamoros by N.S.Jarvis on April 2, 1846 'dressed in a green jacket with red cuffs and collar trimmed with gold lace and wearing a dark brown felt hat with broad brim similar to the one universally worn by the Mexicans.'

Generals' saddlery from the time of independence was probably as specified in the 1840 regulations, with saddle and harness made of black leather with gilt fittings. The dress shabraque was scarlet with two gold bands – the outer 2½in-wide, the inner 1½in – and a Mexican eagle 5in-high embroidered in gold at the corner. The undress item was blue with a 2in-wide gold lace border.

Staff officers

A small General Staff Corps (*Estado Mayor General*) was created on **September 3, 1823**. Initially officers doing staff work attached to head-quarters probably simply wore their regimentals with the added gold

5 F.Lecomte, *Mémoires pittoresques d'un officier de marine* (Paris, 1851) Vol.1, p.530. This incident occurred at Vera Cruz in 1829, when a French warship was standing by to protect its nationals.

aiguillettes that were the distinction of general staff officers in most armies. The same applied to the aides-de-camp of general officers and, predictably, embellishments were subsequently made (see Plate B2).

Following the French intervention at Vera Cruz, a General Staff Corps of the Army (*Plana Mayor del Ejercito*) was created on **October 30, 1838**. All senior generals of divisions and brigades were part of this corps, and could now count on eight adjutant-generals with the rank of colonel, eight lieutenant-colonels as first adjutants, 16 captains, 16 lieutenants and some 'auxiliaries'. From **June 15, 1842**, General Staff officers were assigned a colorful uniform consisting of a scarlet coat with black velvet collar, cuffs, lapels and turn-backs (with three-pointed vertical pocket flaps), a 2in-wide gold lace edging the collar and cuffs, the lapels having eight gold lace buttonhole 'loops' at each side, and gold buttons. The uniform was completed by blue trousers with gold piping, a gold-laced bicorn with tricolor plume for senior officers, and a sword with a green sword knot.

On **September 25, 1844**, the coat facing color was changed to white, the lapels were abolished and the trousers changed to sky-blue. The 'auxiliaries' to the officers of the General Staff Corps had, from **September 28, 1843**, a green coat with crimson collar, cuffs, lapels and turn-backs, an inch-wide gold lace edging the collar, cuffs and lapels, and gold buttons; sky-blue trousers with a gold stripe; a plain bicorn hat, a straight sword with a crimson knot, and crimson horse housings edged with gold.

Garrison staffs (*mayoras de plaza*), headed by town majors, dated from the Spanish administration but were abolished in 1828. This left a void in the municipal administration of cities and major towns which was corrected by a decree of **November 12, 1835** ordering the establishment of garrison staffs. By 1837 town majors had been appointed in Mexico City, Vera Cruz, Campeche, Acapulco, Perote, Santa Ana de Tamaulipas, Matamoros, Monterey (California), San Blas, Guaymas, Merida, Puebla, Oaxaca, Chiapas, San Luis Potosi, Guadalajara, Guanajuanto, Durango, Zacatecas, Tabasco, Morelia, Chihuahua and Leona Vicario. Others

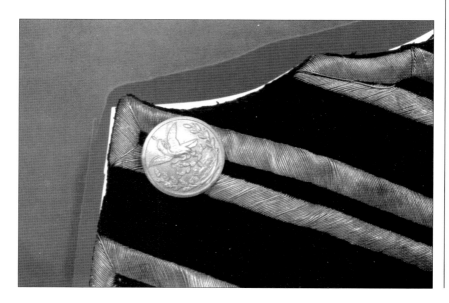

Staff officer's sword, c1820s–1840s. Probably for a junior staff officer, it has a brass guard and mother-of-pearl grip; it may have been imported from either the USA or France. An advertisement in the *Diario del Gobierno de los estados-unidos Mexicanos* of April 3, 1835 announced that parade and campaign swords imported from France were for sale at a shop in Mexico City. (Mr & Mrs Don Troiani Collection)

were added at Queretaro and Baja California in February 1838, and at Aguascaliente, Monterey (Nuevo Leon) and Mazatlan in 1842.

These officers were granted a distinctive uniform in 1835 consisting, for full dress, of a sky-blue coat with blue collar, cuffs and lapels piped scarlet, gilt buttons, gold laced buttonholes, and broad gold lace edging the collar and cuffs; white or blue pantaloons with gold lace, a gold-laced hat with tricolor cockade and scarlet plume. These officers wore gold epaulettes and a red silk waist sash. The undress was basically the same except that the coat had sky-blue lapels and no lace, the blue trousers no lace, and the hat was worn without a plume. This uniform was replaced by the scarlet General Staff uniform introduced in June 1842 (see above).

Administrative officers

These personnel – roughly the equivalent to quartermaster, paymaster, commissary and various other service appointments in the US and British armies – were part of the elaborate and numerous general staff. The first dress regulations were issued on **November 25, 1822**. These called for a green coat with scarlet collar, cuffs and turn-backs, no lapels, and gold buttons; a white waistcoat and trousers, and a laced hat with tricolor cockade and feathers. *Intendentes de Ejercito* (Army Intendants) had an inch-wide gold lace edging the collar, the front, the pocket flaps and the skirts of the coat, with two rows of lace on the cuffs; the waistcoat was also edged with gold lace. *Contadores de Ejercito* (Army Accountants) had the same except for the cuffs, which each bore three embroidered eagles. *Comisarios de Guerra* (Army Commissaries) had the same, but with two eagles on each cuff; and *Tesoreros de Ejercito* (Army Treasurers) had one cuff eagle. Subaltern officers and clerks had basically the same uniforms, but their lace was only a quarter-inch wide and their hats had no feathers. Administrative officers wore no sashes or epaulettes. On **June 8, 1842**, these administrative and accountant officers changed uniform for a blue coat with scarlet collar, cuffs and turn-backs, with the same lace and embroidery as in the 1822 regulations and gold buttons; this was worn with white trousers, and a bicorn without plumes but with a gold cockade loop and tassels. Subaltern officers had quarter-inch silver lace. Artillery and naval administrative officers had the same uniform with gold lace, and the buttons stamped with a grenade or an anchor respectively. At the same date, magistrates of the Military Justice Department were assigned – or possibly confirmed to wear – a single-breasted, long-tailed coat with a waistcoat buttoned to the neck and gold buttons; black trousers, and a bicorn with a black plume and a gold cockade loop. The coat and waistcoat appear to have been black; the coat collar had an elaborate badge at each side – a white circle with a coat of arms in the center and the words *Magistrado Departemental* in a scroll.

CAVALRY

Organization of Permanent regiments

The regiment of Horse Grenadiers of the Imperial Guard had its origin in the mounted escort of Horse Grenadiers attending Gen Iturbide, which already existed in May 1821. As a consequence of Iturbide

becoming emperor the escort became the senior cavalry regiment, initially with some 700 men. In spite of its title, it was a light cavalry unit dressed in hussar uniforms (see Plate B2). It continued as the guard cavalry regiment after Iturbide's fall and the proclamation of the Republic in 1823. On September 10, 1825, it was incorporated into the 2nd Permanent Cavalry Regiment.

The units from which the Permanent (or Line) cavalry regiments were formed from December 24, 1821, came from widely varied backgrounds, some being former regular or provincial Spanish colonial troops while others were revolutionary formations. There were initially 11 numbered regiments; a 12th was formed on March 13, 1822. The 13th, raised on June 26, 1822, was renumbered as the 5th Regiment on December 29, 1826 – the original 5th was disbanded for insubordination and incorporated into the 3rd Regiment on October 16, 1826.

The establishment of each regiment was four squadrons, each of two troops (companies), each troop having a captain, a lieutenant, two cornets, four sergeants, six corporals, two trumpeters, and 56 troopers including eight dismounted. The staff consisted of a colonel, a lieutenant-colonel, two squadron commandants, one captain acting as major, two adjutants (lieutenants), one chaplain, one surgeon, one farrier and two mates, one armorer, one trumpet-major, one corporal and eight pioneers. This total of 614 all ranks on the peace establishment was boosted to 782 when on war footing; but actual strength was usually only about 300–400 men.

Each Line cavalry regiment combined light, heavy and medium cavalry: the 1st Squadron were to be trained as hussars, the 2nd and 3rd as heavy cavalry and the 4th as dragoons. Each company also had 12 men armed with lances, for a theoretical total of 96 lancers per regiment. These lancers seem to have been intended as an elite that could be grouped together when needed.

On **November 19, 1833**, the 12 regiments were consolidated and merged into six regiments having the same establishment as previously. Instead of being numbered, they now assumed the names of notable sieges and battles against the Spanish. The new regiments were organized from the following numbered Line regiments: Dolores – from the 3rd and 6th; Iguala – from 4th and 10th; Cuautla – from 11th and 12th; Vera Cruz – from 5th and 9th; Palmar – from 2nd, 7th and Activo de Mexico; and Tampico, from 1st and 8th.

This lasted until **March 16, 1839**, when the Line cavalry was increased to eight numbered regiments. A 9th Permanent Cavalry Regiment was added in 1841. The number of squadrons remained the same, each squadron having two troops or companies; the companies each had a captain, a lieutenant, two ensigns, one sergeant

13

1st class, four sergeants 2nd class, nine corporals, two trumpeters, and 52 troopers including eight dismounted. The staff consisted of a colonel, a lieutenant-colonel, two squadron commandants, four adjutants (lieutenants), four standard bearers, one chaplain, one surgeon, and 13 enlisted specialists. Light horse units were raised from 1835 and regiments of lancers, cuirassiers and mounted chasseurs were organized in the early 1840s (see below).

Line cavalry uniforms 1821–1840s

On **September 20, 1821**, the Line cavalry was assigned a lemon-yellow coat with scarlet collar, cuffs, turn-backs and piping (without lapels) and white metal buttons; dark gray trousers, and a brass dragoon helmet with a black 'caterpillar' comb. This uniform was common to all 13 Permanent regiments. The regimental distinctions consisted of the regimental number on the buttons, helmet plate and at each side of the collar.

The color of the regular cavalry uniform was changed by an order of **December 6, 1824** to a scarlet coat. By 1826, the cavalry also had blue forage caps, white linen undress jackets and trousers, green housings and green valises, cartridge boxes with brass mountings, and waist belts with brass buckles (see Plate A2). There were many variations, e.g. crested black leather helmets appear to have been much more common than brass. By 1825–26 the cavalry helmets were probably of black leather with white metal plate, crest and visor edging, and horse hair 'tails' are mentioned, which appears to indicate that some units had adopted flowing 'manes' as well as the stuffed crest shown by Linati's prints (see e.g. page 13). It appears from some figures shown in a painting of the battle of Tampico (page 8), that mounted pioneers were distinguished by bearskin caps with white metal plates. The trousers, blue or gray, apparently always had a scarlet stripe. Some cavalry officers seem to have displayed an embroidered palm leaf badge on the collar instead of the regimental number. The **January 2, 1832** clothing contract featured scarlet cavalry coats, as in the 1824 regulations, except that green lapels were added (see Plate D3).

From **July 10, 1839**, each regular cavalry regiment was assigned a distinctive uniform (see below). All regiments had shakos with white metal fittings and lace, all had white metal buttons and, except for the 6th Regiment (which had green), all regiments had blue pantaloons with a scarlet stripe. Housings were all edged with a wide white lace. This regulation was in force only until **August 31, 1840**, when cavalry dress was simplified to one uniform for the whole arm. Henceforth, troopers were to have a sky-blue coat with scarlet collar, cuffs and turn-backs piped in opposite colors, with 2in-high regimental numerals on the collar; dark blue trousers strapped with leather and with an inch-wide scarlet stripe; a

Officer's helmet of 9th Permanent Cavalry Regiment, c1825–33. Black leather with silver furniture, black mane, and tricolor pompon (from outside, green/white/red). The partly visible tuft on the left hand side is green/over white/over red. See Plate A2. (Museo Nacional de Historia, Mexico; author's photo)

Cavalry officer's shako, c1839–48. Black leather with silver plate and lace, tricolor cockade; the chin scales and tuft or plume are missing. (Museo Nacional de Historia, Mexico; author's photo)

tapered shako with white metal plate bearing the national arms and the regimental number, a tricolor cockade and white bands; and sky-blue housings edged with scarlet. However, on **December 22, 1841**, orders were issued for the cavalry to revert to the July 1839 uniforms. According to the 1839/1841 regulations, the dress of each regiment was as follows. Note that in all units except the 9th coats and areas of facing were piped in the opposite color – i.e. for the 1st Regt, scarlet areas were edged with yellow piping, and yellow areas with scarlet piping:

1st Regt: Yellow coat, scarlet collar, cuffs, lapels and turn-backs; scarlet housings. Changed on **September 7, 1845** to: green coatee with green collar and cuffs; yellow lapels, piping and cuff flaps; green epaulettes with scarlet fringes; white metal buttons; gray pantaloons; black leather helmet with yellow metal fittings, black crest and scarlet plume on the left side; blue cape with green collar; scarlet housings edged white (illustrated by G.A. Embleton in MAA 56, *The Mexican-American War 1846–48*).

2nd Regt: Yellow coat, blue collar, cuffs, lapels and turn-backs; blue housings.

3rd Regt: Blue coat, green collar and cuffs, white lapels and turn-backs; green housings.

4th Regt: Sky-blue coat, scarlet collar, cuffs, lapels and turn-backs; green housings.

5th Regt: Blue coat, scarlet collar, cuffs, lapels and turn-backs; scarlet housings.

6th Regt: Green coat, white collar, cuffs, lapels and turn-backs, scarlet cuff flaps; scarlet housings.

7th Regt: White coat, sky-blue collar, cuffs, lapels and turn-backs; green housings.

Rank badges

From **October 16, 1823**, rank badges were to be as follows, metallic lace being in the regimental or corps button color:

Corporal Diagonal stripe of ¼inch yellow or white lace on forearm above cuff.

Second Sergeant The same but in gold or silver lace.

First Sergeant Two such laces.

Sub-Lieutenant One ½inch gold or silver lace around the cuffs.

Lieutenant Two such laces.

Captain Three such laces.

First Adjutant (equivalent to Major) Two gold or silver epaulettes with plain straps

Lieutenant-Colonel The same, with worked straps.

Colonels The same, with star in the opposite metal.

The field officers (first adjutant, lieutenant-colonel and colonel) also had red silk sashes. Regimental officers wore gorgets on duty.

On **January 18, 1830**, the following changes were ordered:

Second Sergeant Epaulette of facing color cloth on right shoulder.

First Sergeant Two such epaulettes.

Sub-Lieutenant Gold or silver epaulette on left shoulder.

Lieutenant The same, but on right shoulder.

Captain Two such epaulettes.

From the same date, rank badges of the **Civic Militia** were made slightly different than those of Permanent and Active Militia troops, as follows:

Second Sergeant Right epaulette with red strap and green fringe for infantry, green strap and red fringe for cavalry.

First Sergeant Two such epaulettes.

Officers Silver straps with gold fringes for infantry, gold straps with silver fringes for cavalry.

8th Regt: Blue coat, scarlet cuffs and lapels, white collar and cuff flaps; green housings.

9th Regt (from December 1841): Green coat, crimson collar, cuffs, lapels and turn-backs, white piping; blue pantaloons with crimson stripe; green housings.

Permanent light cavalry units

From April 28, 1835 the Permanent cavalry was augmented by a Light regiment (*Regimento ligero de Mexico*). It was merged into the new Vera Cruz light cavalry regiment on August 31, 1847.

The Yucatan Squadron (*Escuadron de Yucatan*) was organized from October 16, 1826, and disbanded on December 1, 1847. The Puebla Light Cavalry Squadron (*Escuadron ligero de Puebla*) was raised from October 20, 1841; it merged with other units from December 1, 1847. The Tabasco Permanent Cavalry Company (*Compaña Permanente de Tabasco*) was raised from October 16, 1829, and merged with the Chiapas Active Militia Company to form an unnumbered squadron, disbanded on December 1, 1847. The Isla del Carmen Permanent Cavalry Company (*Compaña Permanente de la Isla del Carmen*), created on October 16, 1829, was disbanded some time in the 1830s.[6]

The initial pre-1835 uniform was probably similar to that of the Permanent cavalry regiments. According to Joseph Hefter, the light cavalry of 1835 was assigned an all medium blue coat with scarlet piping edging the collar, cuffs, turn-backs, pockets and the front; white metal buttons; gray trousers; and a helmet with brass plate, crest and chin scales.[7] From **August 31, 1840**, the uniform of all light cavalry units was ordered to be sky-blue with scarlet trim (see Plate F1).

All this was not quite flamboyant enough for Gen Santa Anna, who was once again at the forefront of Mexico's chaotic politics in the early 1840s. His love of elaborate uniforms led him to raise units of cuirassiers, lancers, hussars (see below and Plate F2) and mounted chasseurs (*Cazadores à caballo*) light cavalry (see illustration page 18).

Cuirassiers

The Mexican army had a most colorful unit of cuirassiers which originated as the Tulancingo Active Militia Squadron raised from June 12, 1840. It was transformed into a heavy cavalry unit as the Tulancingo Cuirassiers (*Coraceros de Tulancingo*) from January 15, 1842. On September 1, 1843, the squadron was made a Permanent unit. It saw action at Angostura, Cerro Gordo, Amozoc, Churubusco and Mexico City before being disbanded on December 1, 1847.

From January 1842 the officers and men were assigned elaborate and distinctive uniforms, one for mounted and another for dismounted service. For mounted duty, officers wore a sky-blue coatee with crimson collar and cuffs, crimson pantaloons (probably with a sky-blue stripe),

Cavalry officer, 1840s. Black shako with silver lace and metal and scarlet pompon; olive green coatee with sky-blue collar, cuffs and lapels; silver buttons and epaulettes, gilt (?) gorget; white trousers with red stripe. (Anne S.K.Brown Military Collection, Providence; author's photo)

6 According to the late Joseph Hefter, *El Soldado Mexicano...*, an 1835 order declared 'some regular and militia units as Light Troops', but the printed legislative collections and the army registers do not specifically mention this. Only the Permanent *Regimento ligero de Mexico* cavalry appears to reflect this order. Some Active Militia units may also have been affected, but this is not stated clearly. All this would seem to indicate that if such an order was issued it was not widely applied.

7 Hefter, *El Soldado Mexicano...*, p.55. We have not found the decree in contemporary sources, but this might have been a unit order not included in the official registers. Regular light infantry units, also said to have been created in 1835, were prescribed an all medium blue coat edged with scarlet piping at collar, cuffs, pockets, turn-backs and down the front; brass buttons; gray trousers; and a shako with brass plate, crest and chin scales, according to Hefter.

A rare image of a trumpeter, 1840, in a sketch by Detmar Finke taken from a painting of Puebla cathedral dated that year. The unit is unknown – the Tulancingo Cuirassiers did not yet exist – but this may be a trumpeter attached to a senior official. It does at least confirm the use of red coats and tasselled chevrons by musicians. Helmet with steel skull and front visor; brass rear visor, edging to front visor, band, front plate, comb and chin scales; red *houpette* from brass base at front of comb; black 'caterpillar' crest with flowing black mane; white/ over red/ over green plume. Red coat with sky-blue collar, cuffs, turn-backs and piping; yellow epaulettes and sleeve chevrons with tassels each end; dark blue trousers. White metal cuirass with brass scale straps; narrow red cloth tied to the white waist belt. (Anne S.K.Brown Military Collection, Providence; author's photo)

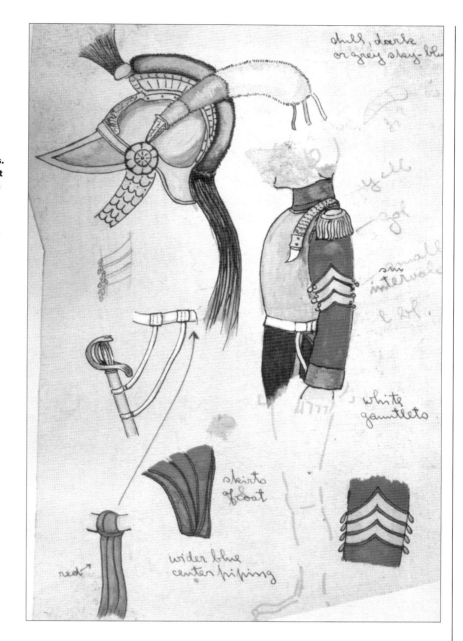

brass cuirass and helmet with silver badges and ornaments, silver belt and cartridge box; sky-blue housings edged with silver lace, and bridles trimmed with silver. When on foot the officers were to wear a sky-blue long-tailed coat with crimson collar and cuffs, sky-blue trousers with a crimson stripe, bicorn hat, boots with spurs, silver cartridge box and belt, and to carry a straight sword.

The NCOs and troopers had a sky-blue coatee with crimson collar, cuffs and piping. When mounted, they wore crimson trousers with a sky-blue stripe and black leather strapping, brass cuirass and helmet trimmed with white metal; the sky-blue housings were edged white, and they were armed with a brass-hilted straight sword and a carbine. When dismounted, NCOs and troopers wore sky-blue trousers with a crimson stripe and boots with spurs. There can be no doubt that the regiment was equipped as a cuirassier unit, from the several trophies now in American museums.

Hussars

The Hussars of the Guard of the Supreme Powers (*Husares de la Guardia de los Supremos Poderes*) originated as an Active Militia light cavalry squadron raised from December 3, 1841, for presidential escort duty in Mexico City. This was only a few weeks after Santa Anna began his sixth presidency, and he wanted guard units; in a Republican regime the Guard Hussars protected the 'supreme powers' held by the president. This unit was augmented by a second squadron, and made a Permanent unit with precedence over all other units on September 1, 1843. It became a regiment on July 27, 1846, when two more squadrons were added. The regiment fought at Angostura, Cerro Gordo, Amozoc, Churubusco, Mexico City and Huamantla. The hussars remained loyal to Santa Anna's government when the five Mexico City National Guard battalions mutinied on February 28, 1847, and Santa Anna rushed them to the city to restore order and rally the guardsmen. The regiment was disbanded on December 1, 1847, a few weeks after Santa Anna had relinquished the presidency and was ordered to give up command of the army. (See Plate F2.)

Lancers

Although there were many troopers armed with lances within Mexican cavalry regiments, the first and only official lancer unit were the Jalisco Lancers (*Lanceros de Jalisco*), an Active Militia unit (see below), raised with two squadrons on July 19, 1843. The Jalisco Lancers, in their red uniforms faced with green, fought at Monterey, Buena Vista and Angostura; when disbanded on December 1, 1847, the remaining lancers were incorporated into other units.

At least one other unit were uniformed as lancers some time before the Mexican War. The Vera Cruz Squadron (*Escuadron de Vera Cruz*) was an Active Militia cavalry squadron raised on August 20, 1823, and often saw active duty, especially as it was from Santa Anna's home area. By the 1840s the Vera Cruz Lancers were dressed in a green lancer uniform faced with scarlet. At the surrender of Vera Cruz (March 29, 1847), George C. Furber saw officers in 'brilliant uniforms of green, trimmed with red' and 'a body of dismounted lancers, dressed in their uniforms of green.' The lancers' remnants were merged into the new Vera Cruz light cavalry regiment on August 31, 1847. Furber also mentioned a body of lancers, apparently a different unit seen in late 1846, that wore 'green uniforms, faced with red and trimmed with yellow.'

In general, lances were popular with Mexican cavalrymen and appear to have been issued to nearly all units in varying numbers. There were officially 12 lancers per company throughout the cavalry arm, but actually a great many more, judging from arms statements and onlookers. In November 1841, Lady Calderon de La Barca noted 'an escort of twenty-three lancers, with a captain, arrived by orders of the governor, Don Panfilo Galiudo, to accompany us during the remainder

Trooper, Jalisco Lancers, 1843–47. The uniform was a scarlet coatee with dark green collar, cuffs and turn-backs, piped in opposite colors; blue trousers with scarlet stripe; lancer cap with red top, black skull, brass plate and yellow cord and plume. The cloak was dark green, the housings dark green edged white, the valise dark green trimmed with scarlet. This uniform was provided, as the Jalisco Lancers were seen in September 1846 at the defense of Monterey, where Albert G.Brackett recalled that a 'large force of Mexican lancers was now seen... they made a most magnificent appearance, dressed... in red and green uniforms... The crimson pennons of their lances fluttered gracefully, while above the rest was the national flag of Mexico; this is a green, white and red tri-color, with the Aztec eagle in the centre.' Reconstruction by J.Hefter. (Anne S.K.Brown Military Collection, Providence; author's photo)

OPPOSITE **Trooper, Mounted Chasseurs, full dress, 1843–47.** Raised on September 20, 1843, the *Cazadores a Caballo* had a fur busby with crimson bag piped white, brass plate and chin scales, and crimson plume; a green coatee with crimson collar, cuffs, cuff flaps, lapels and turn-backs, white lace and piping, white metal buttons; and gray trousers with a crimson stripe. Attached to the Army of the North, the unit distinguished itself at Angostura, attacking the American rearguard. The regiment was amalgamated into the Puebla Light Cavalry in December 1847. Reconstruction by J.Hefter. (Anne S.K.Brown Military Collection, Providence; author's photo)

of our journey. They looked very picturesque, with their lances, and little scarlet flags.' They certainly made an impression on the Americans later on. At Monterey, George C.Furber noted that each trooper was 'armed with a steel-headed lance, about eight feet in length, bearing a small swallow-tailed flag of green and red.' At Buena Vista, S.Compton Smith saw the Mexican cavalry 'most superbly uniformed, and mounted on the choicest horses in the country. Each regiment was distinguished

Officer's helmet, Tulancingo Cuirassiers, c1843–47, probably imported from France. Brass with white metal band bearing a brass flaming bomb; originally this band was covered – except for the badge, no doubt – with jaguar skin. The black mane and tricolor plume are missing. (United States Military Academy Museum, West Point; author's photo)

by the peculiar color of its horses; and… the scarlet pennons of the lancers floated on the morning breeze – with the flags designating the different corps.' At Palo Alto, J.W.McKenzie recalled 'their lances poised, their glittering steel spears in line and their fluttering red pennons looking like long streaks of blood…'

Presidial cavalry companies

On the northern frontier, from Texas bordering the Atlantic Ocean to California on the shores of the Pacific, a chain of permanent Presidial companies of cavalry were posted in the frontier forts called *Presidios,* which had provided a continent-wide buffer zone against hostile Indian incursions since the early 17th century. These forts were often colocated with missions and served as administrative centers. The companies that made up the garrisons were the peculiar 'Cuera' cavalry, so-called because of the protective leather coats and shields used by these mostly Indian-fighting troops. Their duties called for patrols and occasional expeditions against the Indians who were trying to penetrate further south to raid the wealthy ranches in central Mexico. Consequently, they had peculiar arms, equipment and uniforms. Since the mid-18th century there were a few light cavalry 'Volante' companies – so-called because they did not wear the heavy leather coats – posted further south to pursue those intruders that might get through the line of Presidios. From 1826, the Presidial companies in the various states were deployed as follows:

Coahuila and Texas: at Monclava, Agua Verde, Bahia, Rio Grande, Bahia del Espiritu Santo, Béjar, Alamos and Lampazo.

Chihuahua: at Chihuahua town, and the Presidios of San Buenaventura, Janos, San Elzeario, El Norte, Carrizal and Principe.

Sonora and Sinaloa: at Frontera, Tuscon, Altar, Santa Cruz, Buena Vista and Pitic.

New Mexico: at Santa Fe, Bado and Taos.

Alta California and Baja California: at San Francisco, Monterey, Santa Barbara, San Diego, Fronteras and Loreto.

The two 'Volante' companies were in Tamaulipas.

Since 1772, these border Presidial companies had all had basically the same uniform, which was very different from that worn by cavalry in central Mexico. This consisted of a short blue coat with scarlet collar and cuffs, no lapels, brass buttons; blue trousers; a black wide brimmed round hat with a white band, and a blue cloak. The equipment included a cartridge box on a natural leather shoulder belt with the name of the wearer's Presidio on it. The remarkable *cuera* or leather coat was made of several layers of deerskin to provide protection against arrows and lance thrusts. They also carried a leather shield, and were armed with a lance among other weapons.

The transfer from Spanish to Mexican rule in 1822 changed very little in the organization, dress and equipment of the Presidial cavalry (see page 23). From the end of the 1830s, issue records mention variations to the blue jackets. In September 1839 the seven companies in the department of Chihuahua received 102 red coatees. Later on, in December 1844, the company at Lampazos had two red coatees (which may have been for trumpeters); but the two companies in Baja California received 32 red coatees. A year later the two Baja companies reported having 32 canvas jackets, trousers and forage caps. The California companies were also assigned a dress uniform from **January 19, 1842**. This consisted of a blue coat with green collar and cuffs, scarlet lapels and cuff flaps, white piping, and the letters 'AC' (Alta California) or 'BC' (Baja California) at the collar. The blue trousers had a red stripe; a shako with plate and plume was prescribed; and the blue housings were edged with white. The campaign uniform of the California companies remained the blue short coat with scarlet cuffs and collar and the wide-brimmed hat, although the trousers were now specified as gray. There is no indication that all this clothing actually reached these companies. Weapons included carbines, sabers and lances, but none of the Presidial companies reported having pistols or machetes in the early 1840s. For his part, William Preston Stapp recalled that each trooper of the Presidial cavalry who recaptured the Texans of the Mier expedition in the mountains of Coahuila in February 1843 'was armed with a hanger, carbine, and lance, and uniformed in leather jerkins and open pants, with low-crowned wool-hats, ornamented with white bands.'

Active Militia cavalry

The Active Militia cavalry was organized into eight-plus regiments and many squadrons and companies from 1823. They bore the names of their area, e.g. *Regimiento de Puebla, Escuadron de Zacatecas* and *Compania de Acapulco*.

The *Milicia Activa* cavalry had, from **December 6, 1824**, a green coat with scarlet collar, cuffs and turn-backs, green piping edging the collar, cuffs and turn-backs, scarlet piping edging the rest of the coat, and white metal buttons. Other items such as helmets and pantaloons were as the Permanent cavalry. According to Linati, white lace was added on the uniforms imported from England in 1825–26 (see page 24). The green uniform remained in use until **August 31, 1840**, when all units changed to a sky-blue coatee with scarlet collar, cuffs, turn-backs and piping; blue pantaloons with a red stripe and brown leather strapping; a shako, a sky-blue cape, and sky-blue housings edged with red – the same as the light cavalry. By **1843**, this had mostly changed to blue coats, with some units having scarlet coats. In December 1843, the Guarda Costa de Acayucan

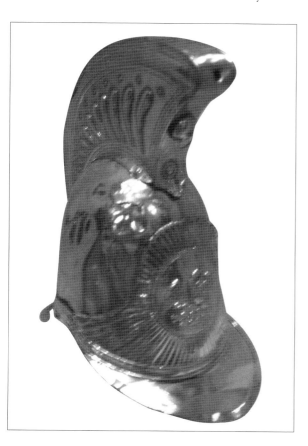

Trooper's helmet, Tulancingo Cuirassiers, c1843–47. Entirely of brass, it was probably made in Mexico. The black mane and the plume are missing. A cuirass in the same collection is of brass with white metal edging; two rivet holes in the chest locate a badge which is now missing – an eagle on rays, as on this helmet. (Missouri History Museum, St Louis; author's photo)

Officer's lance cap, Jalisco Lancers, 1843–47, probably made in France. Black leather skull, square red top with narrow silver piping, silver lace band; silver visor edging, lion masks and chin chain; silver rayed plate with gilt eagle badge. (Museo Nacional de Historia, Mexico; author's photo)

Cavalry Company had 108 red coats. In April 1844, the Guanatajuato Activo Cavalry received 216 red and 216 blue coats; but in 1845 or 1846 only 18 scarlet and 416 blue coats. The Jalapa Squadron was issued only six scarlet coats, but the Chiapas Squadron received five scarlet and 96 blue coats in 1845–46.

The Active Militia Presidial companies on the northern frontier did not wear these uniforms but had the blue jacket and round broad-brimmed hat as the permanent Presidial cavalry companies described above. The Active Militia also had a white warm weather dress, which it apparently wore with the broad-brimmed hat as undress.

Mexican War cavalry uniforms

As there were no further general regulations changing the uniforms of the cavalry between the December 1841 order and 1848, it is usually assumed that this was the dress of the Mexican regular cavalry during the war of 1846–48. While the colorful 1839/1841 regimental uniforms were surely worn by some cavalrymen, at least initially, the reports of the Minister of War to the Mexican Congress reveal many surprising details of the actual issues of cavalry uniforms.

In July and September 1842, blue cloth coats were issued to the 1st Cavalry Regt instead of yellow coats. In 1843, the minister reported the issue of 850 scarlet coats and 5,502 blue coats, along with 3,808 cloth trousers, 3,796 riding pantaloons, 3,800 linen trousers and 4,499 linen jackets. In 1845, the report mentioned 618 scarlet coats and 5,710 blue coats, 5,246 cloth trousers, 4,136 riding pantaloons, 3,257 linen trousers, 4,623 linen jackets and 5,871 shakos with trimmings. This concerned not only the numbered Line regiments of cavalry, but all regular and Active Militia units. The scarlet coats reveal the issue of totally different uniforms than in the 1839/1841 dress regulations. The 9th Cavalry had 20 red and 141 blue coats in August 1842 instead of green; the 2nd Cavalry, 93 red and 12 blue coats in April 1844 instead of yellow; and the 4th, 38 red and 497 blue coats in August 1844 instead of sky-blue.

As Mexico neared war with the United States the Mexican cavalry were clearly being issued substantially different uniforms and equipments from those found in the army dress regulations issued in previous years. In its December 1846 report to the government, the Ministry of War noted that the 1st Cavalry had been issued with 216 scarlet coats instead of yellow; the 3rd, with 127 scarlet coats instead of blue; and the 4th, with 42 scarlet coats and 615 blue coats instead of sky-blue. According to this report, the hussars and the Jalisco Lancers also had a mixture of both scarlet and blue coats. A few other units had large numbers of blue with small numbers of scarlet coats, the latter probably meant for trumpeters. In summary, this 1846 report mentioned the issue of 1,076 scarlet coats and 6,282 blue coats, 3,581 cloth trousers, 5,760 riding pantaloons, 4,911 linen trousers, 4,353 linen jackets and 5,422 shakos with trimmings.

The equipment issued called for: *banderolas* (pennons for lances) 1,034; *morrales* (horse bags) 4,154; *mantas* (horse blankets) 4,112; *chabrases* (shabraques) 243; *mantillas* (horsecloths) 4,292; *mantas de silla* (saddle blankets) 4,250; *maletas* (portmanteaux or valises) 5,125; and *sacos para cebuda* (bags for feed?) 3,934.[8]

Trooper of a Presidial cavalry company, c1826, from a print by Claude Linati. Black hat with white band. Blue coat with red collar, pointed cuffs and turn-backs; raised red crescent shoulder wings centrally striped or piped white; different examples of this print show the cuffs both with and without white piping. White belts and yellow metal; steel scabbard, brass hilt. Gray trousers, black strapping, red stripe. Lance pennon green/ over white/ over red; saddle blanket green, edged white.

F.W.Beechey, a Royal Navy officer visiting California in November 1826, left this description of a typical Presidial cavalryman whom he saw near San Francisco: '... round, blue-cloth jacket, with red cuffs and collar; blue-velvet breeches, which being unbuttoned at the knees, gave greater display to a pair of white cotton stockings, cased more than half the way in a pair of deerskin shoes; a black hat, as broad in the brim as it was disproportionately low in the crown... a profusion of dark hair, which met behind and dangled half way down the back, in the form of a thick cue [sic]. A long musket, with a fox-skin band round the lock, was balanced upon the pommel of his saddle, and he was further provided for defense against [sic] a bull's hide shield, on which was emblazoned the royal arms of Spain, and, by a double-fold of deerskin, carried as a covering over his body. Thus accoutred, he bestrode a saddle, which retained him in his seat by a high pommel in front, and a corresponding one behind. His feet were armed at the heels with a tremendous pair of spurs, secured by a metal chain, and were thrust through an enormous pair of wooden box-shaped stirrups.' (Anne S.K.Brown Military Collection, Providence; author's photo)

8 The 1846 report mentioned blue coats issued to all except the following units: Rgto de Husares – 141 scarlet + 567 blue coats; Lanceros de Jalisco – 108 scarlet + 254 blue; Rgto Ligero – 379 scarlet only; 1o Rgto Cav – 216 scarlet only; 3o Rgto Cav – 127 scarlet only; 4o Rgto Cav – 42 scarlet + 615 blue; Rgto Activo Guanajuato – 18 scarlet + 416 blue; Esc Activo de Jalapa – 6 scarlet only; Esc Activo de Chiapas – 5 scarlet + 96 blue. *Memoria del Ministerio de estada y del despacho de guerra y marina del gobierno supremo de la Republica Mexicana, leida al augusto Congresso nacional el dia 9 de deciembre de 1846 por el general Almonte* (Mexico City, 1846)

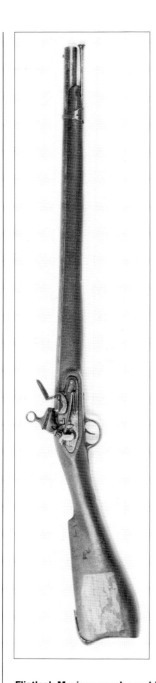

Flintlock Mexican cavalry carbine, c1790–1847. According to the label pasted to the butt, it was captured at the battle of Churubusco in August 1847, and presented to Capt John H.Jackson, 9th US Infantry. The weapon has no maker's marks; Mexico had no arms manufacturers and depended upon imports, especially from Great Britain. However, this piece bears a marked resemblance to late 18th century Spanish carbines; although it conforms to no exact Spanish army model, points of resemblance include the distinctive *miquelet* lock, brass trigger guard and butt plate. The fairly crude wooden stock appears to be of Mexican make with the metal parts fitted locally. (Mr & Mrs Don Troiani Collection)

Trooper, Active Militia cavalry, c1826, wearing a new uniform imported from England. Several British banks, which had loaned money to Mexico and arranged this, improved on the Mexican regulation uniform by adding white tape and buttons – this extra lacing was later omitted. The helmet is black; the coat is green with red cuffs edged white and a white collar edged red (possibly a colorist's error); gray trousers have leather strapping and a red stripe; green saddle cloth and valise are edged white, and there is red binding on the horse's tail. From a print by Claude Linati. (Anne S.K.Brown Military Collection, Providence; author's photo)

Active Militia cavalrymen at Guazacualco, south of Vera Cruz, c1826, from a print by Claude Linati. They wear broad hats and white linen clothing in this tropical region. Some were not as well appointed in January 1832, when they formed part of Santa Anna's rebel army. British visitor Henry Tudor recalled that force as being 'attired in shreds and patches formed of every color of the rainbow. Some had no uniforms... The cavalry, so to call them, were a complete mob of half-starved peasantry... Their accoutrements... corresponded in fanciful variety to the rest of their motley attire; and rusty swords, broken pikes, and worn out firelocks, apparently kept for show rather than use, constituted the mortal weapons of this ragged cavalcade.' (Anne S.K.Brown Military Collection, Providence; author's photo)

Mexican cavalry, 1846–47: detail from 'The Escape of Dan Henrie' by Sam Chamberlain (cf Plate F3). Shako with brass plate, yellow band, red pompon; blue double-breasted coatee, scarlet crescent-shaped wings, yellow metal buttons; blue trousers with scarlet stripe; blue saddle cloth edged red, and red valise; lance with red pennon. Henrie was a scout with the US Army, who narrowly escaped capture by Gen Miñon's cavalry in January 1847. (Anne S.K.Brown Military Collection, Providence; author's photo)

25

These returns thus reveal that regulation uniforms were not followed very closely and that the Ministry of War actually procured simpler uniforms. Obviously a new general issue uniform of blue faced with scarlet had been put in wear in many units from the early 1840s, 1845 at the latest; and possibly a smaller issue of scarlet faced with blue had also been brought forth. This was very different from the official 1839/41 regimental uniforms, but certainly existed in great numbers.

Sam Chamberlain, a US cavalry trooper, left some lively memoirs and watercolors of Mexican cavalry. In January 1847 a party of US cavalry was captured by Gen J.Vincente Miñon's Mexican cavalry brigade; the troopers shown by Chamberlain pursuing the fleeing scout Dan Henrie bear lances and wear blue uniforms with scarlet facings (see page 25). At Buena Vista, Chamberlain recalled with admiration 'their cavalry some six thousand in number was magnificent; these richly caparisoned cavaliers in uniforms of blue faced with red, with waving plumes and glittering weapons advanced towards us…' His watercolors show some cavalry in blue, seemingly single-breasted coatees with scarlet collar, cuffs, turn-backs and shoulder tabs (for holding epaulettes), sky-blue trousers with scarlet stripe, and tapered shakos with brass plate and chin scales and red pompons. Only in the 1848 dress regulations is this uniform specifically ordered, but it is obvious that it had been in use for years previously.

To confuse the issue still further, there were parts of regiments dressed in the 1839/41 regulation uniform. This appears to have been the case with the 9th Cavalry, reported with blue coats in 1842, but also seen by Brackett in 1846 wearing 'conical-shaped leather caps [shakos], with little red balls in the top'; and some cavalry that 'wore green coats, and blue pants trimmed with red' were obviously in the 9th's 1841 regulation uniform. Some others, notably Civic Militia/National Guard troops, were supplied by local governments; hence the variety, such as green lancer uniforms, noted by American observers. Their overall observations, however, confirm the issue reports to the effect that the Mexican cavalry usually wore blue faced with scarlet, with the shako (see Plate F3).

INFANTRY

Organization of Permanent regiments

From November 1821 the Permanent infantry of the line consisted of 13 regiments of two battalions each; but this was reduced in 1823 to 12 single-battalion regiments, which were often also termed 'battalions' from that date. There was also a short-lived Regiment of Imperial Grenadiers formed on November 7, 1821, and disbanded in October 1823 when Mexico became a republic. From May 1824, each battalion was organized in one company of grenadiers, one company of voltigeurs, and six companies of fusiliers. Each of the battalion's eight companies had an establishment of a captain, a lieutenant, two ensigns, four sergeants, ten corporals, three buglers/drummers and 83 privates. The staff consisted of a colonel, a lieutenant-colonel, two adjutants, one standard-bearer, one chaplain, one surgeon, one armorer, one bugle-major, one drum-major, one paymaster, one bugle-corporal, one corporal and eight pioneers. Battalion establishment thus totaled 823 in peacetime, expanded to 1,223 when on a war footing; but the actual strength was always far lower, hovering around 500 to 600 men.

On **November 19, 1833**, the number of Permanent regiments was reduced to ten. Previously, regiments had been known only by their numbers; now they were given the names of heroes of the cause of independence: Hidalgo, Allende, Morelos, Guerrero, Matamoros, Aldama, Abasolo, Jimenez, Galeana and Landero. This lasted until **March 16, 1839**, when the infantry was augmented to 12 numbered, two-battalion regiments. The eight-company battalion organization was unchanged, each company having a captain, a lieutenant, two sub-lieutenants, one sergeant 1st class, four sergeants 2nd class, nine corporals, one drummer, one bugler, one fifer (or four buglers in the light company) and 80 privates. The regimental staff consisted of a colonel, a lieutenant-colonel, a commandant (major) for the 2nd Bn, one sub-lieutenant standard-bearer, two chaplains, two surgeons, one drum-major, one bugle-corporal, two corporals and 16 pioneers, and two armorers. Besides the regiments, the Permanent infantry also included eight independent infantry companies, and a battalion of Invalids (pensioners) in Mexico City.

From 1840, three numbered battalions of **light infantry** were raised; a 4th was added in 1846 by converting the 1st Bn, 3rd Line Infantry Regiment. The battalion of Grenadiers of the Guard of the Supreme Powers was raised from October 1841; and the *Fijo de Mexico* battalion in 1843.

Most Line infantry units were dissolved or wiped out in 1847, the survivors being formed into

Infantry in white warm weather dress, c1826, trimmed with red collar, cuffs, wings, and a band at the bottom of the jacket. The white shako cover has a red band and tie at the bottom and a tricolor cockade, shown as green/ red/ white reading inwards. His accoutrements are white, and he seems to wear straw-colored sandals. (Anne S.K.Brown Military Collection, Providence; author's photo)

20 temporary battalions on December 20, 1847, and into eight regiments in November 1848.

Active Militia infantry

Milicia Activa units had the same organization as the Permanent troops and were known by the name of their city or state, e.g. *Batallon Activo de Tres Villas*. They formed an important part of the army; in 1826 their establishment called for 20 battalions. With eight cavalry regiments and many independent companies, this gave a theoretical total of 42,000 men, while the Permanent units' establishment numbered 22,750.

In June 1840 the infantry was reorganized into three two-battalion regiments numbered 1 to 3; eight battalions numbered 4 to 11; and eight independent companies. A few further units were formed in the following years. All Active Militia units were dissolved or incorporated into the regular army from December 1, 1847.

The Spanish **Coast Guard Militia** was reorganized into 13 battalions from August 20, 1823. Each had six fusilier companies, each with a captain, a lieutenant, two sub-lieutenants, one first and four second sergeants, six first and six second corporals, two drummers, a fifer, a bugler, and the 'appropriate number' of privates. The permanent staff consisted of a commandant, a quartermaster captain, two adjutant lieutenants and a drum-major. From 1839, the establishment was the same as the Permanent infantry. Battalions bore the names of their areas, and several more were added from 1840. All were dissolved in December 1847.

Irish-American deserters were formed into the two-company **San Patricio Legion** in July 1847; almost destroyed in August, it was disbanded in 1848.

Infantry uniforms

The dress of the soldiers serving in the Permanent and embodied Active Militia units was identical from 1821 until 1839. This was based on the principle of having a single uniform per arm of service, as in the French, Spanish and American infantry, rather than having distinctive regimental uniforms as in the British and certain German armies.

On **September 20, 1821**, the uniform of the infantry was ordered to be a blue single-breasted coat without lapels, with scarlet collar, cuffs, turn-backs and piping and brass buttons; dark gray or white linen trousers; and a shako with brass plate

and chin scales. The regimental number was to appear on the buttons, shako plate and collar. The uniforms bought in 1825 were as above, except that the trousers were blue. There were also some 7,600 blue frock coats for undress wear, called *levitas* in Mexico. There were various detail differences and exceptions to this generic description, but by and large it was the standard uniform until **January 1832**.

In that month the government contracted for 10,000 infantry uniforms which added scarlet lapels, and white (instead of scarlet) piping to edge the collar, cuffs, lapels and turn-backs. The coat tails were probably long, as was now the fashion in France and Britain. This important but exceptional specification was abolished on **June 13, 1833**, when orders were issued to make the uniforms henceforth without lapels, and piped scarlet as per regulations.

Many details could vary. Shakos followed the French styles of the day. They are shown either plain or, in the mid-1820s, with yellow bands at top and bottom. In the late 1820s a famous Linati print (reproduced here) shows a green, white and red roundel on top. R.M.Potter recalled that in Texas in 1836 their 'head dress was the old fashioned black shako of leather or felt, bearing the usual pompon & metallic trimmings & such as letter and number. It often had drawn over it, a close fitting white cloth cover with the decorations outside. Worsted shoulder knots [probably meaning epaulettes] of red, blue, or green were worn by some battalions.' Some grenadiers had three pointed-end laces on the cuffs and lower sleeves. Sappers are shown in the 1820s with bearskin caps and aprons.

In Texas, officers 'seldom appeared in coats except on dress parade. Their costume for march and action was a blue cloth jacket, frogged and braided, with pantaloons to match or white, with an ordinary

'Guard at the Fort of Campeche', c1827. The torrid climate of the Yucatan peninsula would have made standing guard in a heavy cloth uniform unbearable; this soldier, from a print after Frederick Waldeck, wears a straw hat and sandals, and a linen shirt and rolled trousers; his accoutrements are black. (Anne S.K.Brown Military Collection, Providence; author's photo)

sombrero for headgear. On fatigue they wore epaulettes or shoulder straps according to caprice, but always one or the other. The forage cap, occasionally worn by officers and men, had a peak which hung with a tassel at the point.' The soldiers also had a cloth fatigue cap, usually of the French 'turban and flame' shape, in blue piped with red. The undress *levita* frocks appear to have been little used in the 1830s. For cold weather, infantrymen might be issued with an overcoat of coarse blue wool cloth. This was only theoretically general issue; in February 1836, during the Texas campaign, a few men of a battalion from tropical Yucatan died from exposure for lack of warm clothing.

The men were mostly armed with British India Pattern flintlock muskets with bayonets; the elite companies, gunners and sappers, corporals and sergeants also had, in principle, brass-hilted hangers. White cross belts supported the cartridge box and the bayonet (and hanger, where issued). A small brass belt plate is sometimes shown, with attached brush and picker. The knapsacks were of goat hide with the hair outside, a gray blanket or blue greatcoat being rolled on top. Again, variations occurred; e.g., black cross belts might be worn with the white cotton uniform on campaign. Round canteens were sometimes available, made of tin and stamped with the Mexican eagle.

The law of **July 10, 1839** specified radically new uniforms that were based on regimental distinctions. These were changed back to the single arm-of-service uniform on **August 31, 1840.** The blue coat had a scarlet collar, cuffs, cuff flaps and piping, a yellow/gold regimental number at the collar, and brass buttons; sky-blue trousers had scarlet piping; shakos, a brass plate bearing the national arms and regimental number, tricolor cockade and yellow bands. The shako pompon and epaulettess were to be crimson for fusiliers, grenadiers, light infantrymen and pioneers alike. On **December 22, 1841**, the regimental type uniform ordered two years earlier was once again ordered to be implemented (1st and 3rd Regts illustrated by G.A.Embleton in MAA 56, *The Mexican-American War 1846–48*). The coats and trousers were blue (white in summer), with brass buttons. The distinctions were:

1st Regt: Scarlet collar, cuffs and cuff flaps, yellow lapels and piping.

2nd Regt: Sky-blue collar, scarlet lapels, cuffs, cuff flaps and piping.

3rd Regt: Sky-blue collar and piping, crimson lapels, cuffs and cuff flaps.

4th Regt: Sky-blue collar and cuffs, scarlet lapels and cuff flaps, white piping.

5th Regt: Sky-blue cuffs and piping, scarlet collar, lapels and cuff flaps.

6th Regt: Crimson collar, cuffs and cuff flaps, white lapels, piping in opposite colors.

7th Regt: Green collar and cuffs, crimson lapels, cuff flaps and piping, yellow/gold buttonhole loops.[9]

8th Regt: Scarlet collar and cuffs, sky-blue lapels and cuff flaps, piping in opposite colors.

9th Regt: Buff collar and cuff flaps, purple lapels and cuffs, piping in opposite colors.

10th Regt: Scarlet collar and cuffs, purple lapels and cuff flaps, buff piping.

---

9 Secondary sources have usually shown the 7th to be without lapels; contemporary sources consulted all mention *solapas* (lapels). For all regiments, *barras* is interpreted as cuff flaps, but could also be the color of the turn-backs.

11th Regt: Scarlet collar, cuffs and cuff flaps, green lapels.

From December 22, 1841: White coat with sky-blue collar, cuffs and lapels, scarlet cuff flaps and piping; scarlet trousers with scarlet stripe – changed on June 30, 1842, to crimson trousers with white stripe.

12th Regt: Buff collar, lapels and cuffs, scarlet cuff flaps, piping in opposite colors.

The 1840s reforms

Although not specified in detail in any Mexican dress regulation, the great changes to French uniforms during the early 1840s obviously had a profound effect in Mexico. The French infantry, following its experiences in Algeria, went from the old swallow-tailed coat to a style termed the *tunique*. This garment had an easier fit for more comfort and, instead of the front rounded off at the waist and knee-length tails turned back behind the legs, it had a full skirt to the knees all round. It usually had a single row of buttons in front, but might have two or even three rows. The other major change was to the formerly cylindrical shako, which now became tapered and with its rear profile sloping forward. The Mexican military, always eager to follow the latest fashions, tried out the new uniform soon after it was introduced in France.

Just as in France, this fashion was first introduced to light infantry units. In 1843 the Misto Battalion, redesignated the 3o Regimiento Ligero on November 7, was the only unit reporting 800 each of *levitas, casacas y pantalons de paño* (tunic-style coats, tailcoats and trousers of cloth). That same year contracts were let to make some 13,000 uniforms for the army, and some of these must have been for more tunic-style *levita* coats, tailcoats and shakos which would have been issued during 1844. These *levitas* would have been more finished than the undress frocks also called *levitas* in the 1820s. The new tunic-style *levita* coats

(continued on page 41)

Officers of lancers and infantry, 1840s – images in a guide to sword drill. This lancer (left) has a cap with a dark green top, crimson plume, and silver plate; a dark green coatee with crimson cuffs and lapels – the collar is obscured, but silver-laced; silver epaulettes, gorget and buttons; and light gray trousers with a crimson stripe. The infantry officer's black shako has gilt furniture and a white pompon; his blue French-style frock coat has sky-blue cuffs and lapels, coat-color blue collar, gold epaulettes, gorget and buttons; his trousers are white. Other images in this sequence show a lancer officer in a red uniform faced light green, with yellow plume; and an infantry officer in the old round-waisted, long-tailed blue coat, faced light green with red piping, and sky-blue trousers. (Anne S.K.Brown Military Collection, Providence; author's photo)

CALACUERDA

REGULAR & ACTIVE MILITIA CAVALRY, 1820s–1830s
1: Colonel, Moncada Dragoon Regt, 1821
2: Officer, 9th Permanent Cavalry Regt, c1824–33
3: Field officer, Active Militia cavalry, 1824–33

WRy. 03

A

INFANTRY & STAFF, 1820s–1830s
1: Fusilier, infantry, 1826
2: ADC detached from Horse Grenadiers Regt, 1821–23
3: Comisario de Guerra, undress, 1820s–1830s

B

WRY. 03

INFANTRY & ARTILLERY, 1820s–1830s
1: Drummer, infantry, c1830
2: Private, 3rd Permanent Infantry Regt, c1830
3: Gunner, Corps of Artillery, 1820s–1830s

1

2

3

WRY. 03

C

LINE INFANTRY & CAVALRY, 1830s
1: First Sergeant, Hidalgo Inf Regt, c1832–36
2: Grenadier, infantry, summer dress, c1836–38
3: Trooper, Permanent cavalry, c1832–36

1

2

3

WRY. 03

D

CALIFORNIA, 1830s–1840s
1: Trooper, Presidial cavalry, Lower California, c1839
2: Officer, Fijo de California Bn, 1842–47
3: Trooper, Militia cavalry, 1846–47

WRY. 03

E

CAVALRY, 1839–46
1: Trooper, Light Cavalry, 1840–46
2: Trooper, Husares de la Guardia de los Supremos Poderes, 1843–46
3: Trooper, cavalry uniform, c1845–48

F

WRY. 03

INFANTRY, 1839–47
1: First Sergeant, 4th Light Infantry Regt, 1846–47
2: Fusilier, Fijo de Mexico Bn, 1843–47
3: Officer, Active Militia, 1842–47

WRY. 03

G

DEFENCE OF MEXICO CITY, 1847
1: Fusilier, Bravos National Guard Bn
2: Officer, San Blas Active Militia Coast Guard Bn
3: Cadet, Military College, service dress

WRy. 03

were clearly winning favor among the Line as well as the Light infantry, since by March 1845 there were 10,895 cloth *levitas* issued – an enormous increase within two years. There were also 8,975 cloth coats, 10,213 cloth trousers, 12,378 stocks, 18,734 linen jackets and 20,453 linen trousers. For headwear there were 12,550 shakos with trimmings and 11,301 forage caps. Perhaps the most surprising figure was that there were only 6,015 pairs of shoes; this seems to indicate that most of the ordinary infantrymen wore sandals.

In November 1846 the infantry had 11,855 cloth *levitas*, 12,503 shakos with trimmings, 10,968 cloth coats, 10,012 cloth trousers, 15,241 linen jackets, 17,258 linen trousers, 11,934 stocks, 8,549 forage caps and 6,318 pairs of shoes. Thus, less than half of the infantry now had the older style coats with turn-back tails, while over half wore the tunic-style *levitas*. These new coats appear to have had collars and cuffs – and occasionally lapels – of contrasting colors. The white linen jackets meant for hot weather were often the only jacket a soldier might see, especially for troops posted on the Gulf coast and in the tropical Yucatan peninsula. The color of the trousers also varied; they were usually of blue cloth or white linen, but illustrations occasionally show gray, sky-blue, and even red trousers like the French Line infantry.

Independent companies had the same uniform as the Line until **January 18, 1842**, when they were assigned a blue coat with scarlet collar, cuffs and piping, and the initial of the unit's area on the collar, e.g. 'T' for Tampico. Coast Guard Militia units had the same uniforms as the Active Militia. For Active Militia uniforms, see commentary to Plate G3.

Light infantry

The light or *Ligero* regiments were some of the most loyal and favored of Santa Anna's troops, and consequently were among the best clothed units in the army. They had precedence over all other infantry units except the 1st Regiment. The 1st Light Regiment was raised on July 15, 1840; the 2nd on July 28, 1843; the 3rd on November 8 that year; and the 4th in March 1846. In December 1847 the Light regiments were converted into Line infantry.

The uniform of the 1st in 1840 was an all blue coat edged with scarlet piping and with brass ball buttons, with a yellow 'L' (for Ligero) on the right side of the collar and 'P' (for Primero) on the left; gray trousers with scarlet piping, and a gray greatcoat. The shako was lower than the Line type, with black leather bands and chin strap, brass bugle horn badge in front, a tricolor cockade and green pompon. Accoutrements were black leather, without a belt plate. For campaign and fatigues a gray round jacket and trousers piped with scarlet were issued. The regiment also had the *levita* tunic.

The 2nd and 3rd Regiments had the same uniform, the 3rd having the *levita* tunic and its grenadiers bearskin caps. For the 4th Light Infantry uniform, see Plate G1 and illustrations.

The Guard Grenadiers

Mexico twice had a regiment of Guard Grenadiers between 1821 and 1847. The first was formed on November 7, 1821, under the name of *Granaderos Imperiales*. This two-battalion regiment, 500 strong, was formed with men from the grenadier companies of the Guadalajara and

Infantry officer, 1840s. Black shako with gold lace and metal, scarlet pompon. Blue tail-coat with sky-blue collar and cuffs, scarlet turn-backs; gold buttons, epaulettes and turn-back badge; white trousers. (Anne S.K.Brown Military Collection, Providence; author's photo)

Comercio de Mexico militia regiments. In December 1822, Gen Santa Anna, commanding the troops in Vera Cruz, rose against the Emperor Augustin (Iturbide) and marched on Jalapa. On the way his troops captured a detachment of Imperial Grenadiers, most of whom switched sides. They deserted again while Santa Anna's force was attacking Jalapa. By 1823 the revolt was spreading, and in the finest Praetorian tradition some of the regiment were involved in plots to depose the emperor they were supposed to guard. Following the fall of Augustin I the regiment was dissolved, and its officers and men formed the reorganized 1st Line Infantry on October 11, 1823. Lucas Alaman recalled the regiment as having scarlet uniforms.

As mentioned above regarding the Hussars of the Guard, when Santa Anna came back to power for the sixth time late in 1841 he got around the difficulty of the Republican tradition by ordering the creation of household units to guard the 'supreme powers of the presidency' rather than merely the president's person. Formed on December 7, the Battalion of Grenadiers of the Guard of the Supreme Powers (*Batallon de Granaderos de la Guardia de los Supremos Poderes*) was supposed to have 1,200 men divided into eight companies, but the actual strength appears to have been only about 300 officers and men. Nevertheless, it was predictably one of Santa Anna's favorite units and was consequently well equipped with superb uniforms. The grenadier battalion was dissolved in July 1845 soon after Santa Anna temporarily lost power; upon his return to office the unit was re-raised, with some 500 men in September 1846. The grenadiers of this elite corps gave a very good account of themselves in combat during the war with the United States, notably at Cerro Gordo and in the final campaign in the valley of Mexico City. The remnants of the unit retreated to Queretaro following the fall of the capital, and were disbanded there on December 1, 1847, the officers and men being incorporated into the battalion of sappers.

The first uniform of the grenadiers consisted of a blue coat with sky-blue collar with a black collar patch, black cuffs, yellow lace buttonholes, yellow epaulettes and brass buttons; blue trousers, a bearskin cap, and a shoulder belt plate with the name of the unit. On **September 9, 1842**, the uniform was changed to a scarlet coat with sky-blue collar, cuffs and turn-backs (a yellow grenade on each turn-back), white lapels and piping, yellow buttonhole lace and brass buttons;

three-pointed pocket flaps on the coat tails; sky-blue trousers with yellow piping; and a bearskin cap with a plate showing a grenade. The regiment must have received this uniform, as it had 599 bearskin caps according to an 1845 report. This was the dress uniform (illustrated by G.A. Embleton in MAA 56, *The Mexican-American War 1846–48*); for undress and field duty, a blue *levita* and shako were worn. The 1846–47 uniform of the reconstituted regiment is uncertain, but was most likely the blue *levita* tunic-style coat with a shako.

The Californias Battalion

This battalion had a short existence but an intriguing history. It was authorized by a decree of January 8, 1842, to serve in the Alta California (the present American state of California), where the central government wished 'to defend the territory which was threatened with invasion on the part of adventurers or immigrants who had entered the country in great numbers.' José Maria Almador, a native of California, recalled that it was meant to be a 'first class' unit, but unfortunately the government ended up sending a 'hastily formed battalion which was for the most part composed of profligates, men recruited from the prisons', along with 'a considerable number of officers' who had been 'honored with imprisonment for life.'

In late 1842 the new governor, BrigGen José Mariano Micheltorenas, arrived at San Diego with the 500-strong Californias Battalion and, after 'disciplining this horde to some extent', marched on towards Monterey, Alta California's capital. While he was at San Fernando, news of US Commodore Jones' hasty seizure of Monterey reached Micheltorenas. He met Jones, a satisfactory understanding was reached, and the American sailors left. The Californians were upset at seeing the authority of the central government enforced by jailbirds and, by 1843, there had been several encounters (though with no casualties except for 'some of the animals'). After discussions with local leaders, Micheltorenas and his battalion of jailbirds sailed in 1845 for Mazatlan in Baja California. The California Battalion remained there, somewhat forgotten, until November 10–11, 1847, when, with a few other troops in garrison, it surrendered to the landing parties of an American naval force which captured the town. The battalion was disbanded on January 11, 1848. (See Plate E2).

An intriguingly different image of an infantry officer, 1840s. Blue soft cap, black visor; blue French-style frock coat, scarlet cuffs and three-point collar patch; gold epaulettes and buttons; white trousers. There appear to be three rows of buttons on the chest, with lines of transverse lace; scarlet edge piping on the three-point horizontal pocket flap; and gold edging to the collar and cuffs. (Anne S.K. Brown Military Collection, Providence; author's photo)

TECHNICAL TROOPS

Corps of Artillery

As with other branches of the army, the artillery originated from the professional corps of the Spanish colonial military establishment. Spain had maintained an adequate number of gunners in New Spain with a good cadre of professionally educated officers. Independence in 1821 found Mexico with a sizeable artillery park, including guns mounted in the many forts as well as field batteries. These guns consisted mostly of the Spanish version of France's Gribeauval system of artillery (see New Vanguard 66, *Napoleon's Guns 1792–1815(1))*, as expressed in Morla's excellent *Tratado de Artilleria* which remained the basic reference work for any artillery officer in independent Mexico.

By 1822 the Permanent artillery was organized into six foot companies, two horse companies and a few garrison companies. From February 14, 1824, the National Artillery Corps was officially established. It had three brigades: two of foot artillery with an establishment of 1,178 men, and one of horse artillery with 589 men. In 1824–26 there were 11 companies of Active Militia garrison artillery totaling 1,152 men. The most important action of the Mexican gunners was in 1825 at Vera Cruz, where the Spanish still held the island fortress of San Juan de Ulloa. In early January the Mexican gunners opened up on vessels supplying the fortress and sank an American schooner. The blockade tightened and bombardment intensified; in October, the gunners had furnaces built so they could fire heated shot; Congreve rockets were also used. The trapped garrison finally surrendered and evacuated the

Shako of an officer of grenadiers or artillery, c1840. Black leather with gilt flaming bomb badge, rosettes and chin scales; gold lace lower band, cockade loop and pompon base; red top band and pompon; tricolor cockade, reading inwards red/ white/ green. (Museo Nacional de Historia, Mexico)

fortress on November 19, 1825, thus putting an end to over three centuries of Spanish presence in Mexico. This was probably the high point of the Mexican artillery's early history.

Nevertheless, there were relatively few knowledgeable and well trained artillery officers. In 1826–27, General (later President) José Joaquin de Herrera was director of the corps; he put special emphasis on training, and opened two gunpowder mills, but little was done after his departure. Funds for the corps were scarce and, from November 1833, the horse artillery brigade was suspended. There were attempts to improve the army's professional services from 1840. During the early 1840s the artillery corps establishment rose to 266 officers and 4,989 men, organized into three battalions (or foot brigades) each having six batteries of six guns; a horse artillery brigade of eight batteries each with six guns; nine independent garrison companies, three artificer companies, and two train companies. Despite this impressive 'paper' strength, in November 1846, while war was raging with the United States, the corps' actual strength was only 166 officers and 1,957 men. Support personnel consisted of a few arsenal officers and accounting officials with about 200 clerks and arsenal workmen. In December 1843 the creation of a special school for artillery and engineer officers had been officially ordered, but it was never actually established for lack of money.

There had been militia artillery during the Spanish regime, and a decree of May 3, 1823, creating the *Milicia Nacional de Artilleria* continued this establishment. The companies were based in the larger provincial towns and seaports; Mexico City had a brigade of militia artillery. Each company had about 50 men led by a captain, a lieutenant and sub-lieutenant; they were to be trained by regular artillery personnel.

From the time of independence until the war with the United States in 1846, the guns of the Mexican field artillery were largely the ageing Spanish brass 4-, 6-, 8- and 12-pdrs mounted on Gribeauval carriages. In 1846 there were only about 150 field guns fit for service; but the quality of these was generally good, although some few might have honeycombed chambers due to age. There was a good arsenal in Mexico City for the maintenance of the pieces and the manufacture of carriages. Until the 1840s guns were not cast in Mexico, and when brass cannons were cast locally in 1846 their quality proved disappointing.

If most of the guns and carriages equaled those of the American field artillery, which was also based on the Gribeauval system, the same could not be said of their ammunition and train. Mexican black powder was usually coarse and of bad quality, with a consequently low propellant efficiency. Cannonballs were adequate, but more complicated ammunition tended to be of bad quality: grape shot, for example, was so poorly made that its range was considerably reduced. After the horse brigade was suspended at the end of 1833 there was no fast-moving field artillery, despite some seemingly failed attempts to

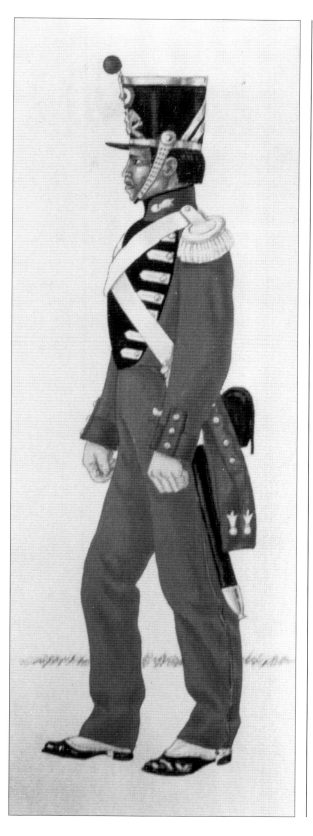

Gunner, Corps of Artillery, full dress according to the regulations of August 31, 1840. The artillery was assigned a black shako with yellow lace bands, brass plate and scales, crimson pompon and tricolor cockade. The full dress blue coat had crimson collar, cuffs, turn-backs and piping; black lapels with seven yellow laced buttonholes; yellow epaulettes; brass buttons; and double vertical pockets to each coat tail. The collars bore a yellow embroidered flaming bomb with numerals – 1 to 4 for brigades, 1 to 5 for independent companies; turn-backs bore double flaming bomb ornaments. For ordinary duty foot artillerymen were to have a blue greatcoat with a crimson collar bearing the embroidered bomb and unit number. Gunners were armed with muskets and bayonets in addition to the sidearm illustrated; the cartridge box bore a brass badge. Reconstruction by J.Hefter. (Anne S.K.Brown Military Collection, Providence; author's photo)

Mexican gunners being ridden down by US cavalry led by Capt May at Resaca de la Palma on May 9, 1846, in a late 19th century plate by American illustrator Henry Ogden. A pioneer student of uniforms, Ogden portrays the gunners surprisingly well, in the *levita* tunic which the artillery seem to have preferred double-breasted, white trousers and gaiters. The shakos seem somewhat too tapered here; and the cuffs may also have been squared, or finished with a cuff flap.

reorganize it during the 1840s. As for the train, it did not truly exist. Ammunition wagons consisted of carts that were rented when needed. Moving the guns was a daunting challenge as Mexican horses were light and frisky, thus lacking the necessary pulling power of bigger beasts bred for draft. In any event, there were no artillery train units devoted to the task, and the movement of guns was done by private contractors using atrociously slow ox or mule teams. Once on a battlefield, the guns tended to stay in one position, since it was next to impossible to move them around quickly. Tolerable during Mexico's endemic civil wars, these shortcomings put the Mexican armies at great disadvantage when facing the US Army, which had good quality powder and ammunition, heavy horses, trained drivers and fast-moving light batteries.

There were also some brass Spanish 16- and 24-pdrs for garrison and siege artillery, although the elaborate Gribeauval traversing platforms seem to have been rarely (if ever) present in Mexican forts. Forts had collections of older guns of brass or iron, usually Spanish but some few might be foreign – for instance, a few French pieces dating back to Louis XIV's reign could be found in the forts defending Puebla. On the other hand, gunners at Vera Cruz had Congreve rockets and some 70 British heavy iron guns, including many 32-pdrs and 24-pdrs.

Artillery uniforms

Information on the uniforms of Mexican artillery is somewhat sketchy before 1840 (see Plate C3). By the regulations of **August 31, 1840**, the artillery uniform became much more elaborate, with a full dress (see page 45) and ordinary duty dress.

In practice, the usual uniform was the skirted tunic-style coat. Surviving paintings made during the Mexican War indicate that some gunners had blue tunic-style coats with crimson collar and cuffs. This is confirmed by 1846 documents showing that artillery stores had 224 *levitas,* together with 608 cloth coats and 493 cloth trousers, as well as 707 shakos with trimmings, 747 garrison caps, 557 greatcoats, and linen smocks and trousers. At Chapultepec in 1847, Capt Mayne Reid saw 'the parapet crowded with Mexican artillerists, in uniform of dark blue with crimson facings, each musket in hand, and all aiming, as I believed, at my own person.' A surviving officer's frock coat is cut after the French style, with two rows of breast buttons (making blue lapels), a crimson collar bearing a gold flaming bomb (but no number), and crimson piping edging the cuffs, cuff flaps, lapels and pocket flaps (illustrated by G.A. Embleton in MAA 56, *The Mexican-American War 1846–48*).

Detail from a painting by J.Escalante of artillery at the battle of Molino del Rey on September 8, 1847. Most of the gunners wear a tailless blue 'round' jacket with crimson collar and cuffs, white or blue trousers with a crimson stripe, and a shako with a white turban and red pompon. Accoutrements are a rectangular black knapsack with mess tin and medium blue blanket roll, and white belts. The brass guns appear to be old Spanish Gribeauvals, but the carriages are new, with single block trails. (Museo Nacional de Historia, Mexico; author's photo)

By the August 1840 regulations, the horse artillery was to have the same uniform as the foot but with short-tailed coatees rather than long-tailed coats, with a 1½in lace edging the cuffs and three ½in diagonal laces on each sleeve. This was worn with trousers strapped with leather, boots, white buckskin gauntlet gloves, and a blue cape with crimson collar; horse housings were blue with a 2in crimson lace edging. Officers had gold buttons, lace and epaulettes. The 1846 lists also mentioned various items peculiar to horse artillery (usually 150 to 200 in number), such as sabers, saber belts, carbines, saddle blankets, bridles, and 14 trumpets.

The 1840 regulations also specified uniforms for various support personnel of the artillery corps. Arsenal and factory personnel were to have a blue jacket piped crimson, with crimson collar bearing the corps insignia, brass buttons, blue trousers, and a black round hat with the corps insignia in front. Arsenal officers had the same uniform as battery officers. Artillery accounting officials had a simple blue single-breasted coat with wide skirts, seemingly of tunic style, with a gold flaming bomb at the collar, gold lace edging

Posthumous portrait of Lieutenant Juan de la Barrera of the Zapadores, who was killed aged 19 during the defense of Chapultepec Castle, Mexico City, on September 13, 1847. The gold lace edging the collar and lapels, single epaulette, and a distinctive Sapper Battalion left sleeve badge are all shown, but the artist has omitted the lapel buttons. Note the pointed lace loops on the crimson cuff. (Museo Nacional de Historia, Mexico; author's photo)

the collar and cuffs and, for senior officials, embroidery similar to that ordered for intendants and commissaries in December 1822 (see above).

Engineers and *Zapadores*
In March 1822, Gen D.Diego Garcia formed the Corps of Engineers which, in 1825, had a director, three lieutenant-colonels, four captains, two lieutenants, and 18 sub-lieutenants. However, there were persistent difficulties in recruiting qualified officers. The enlisted men were in the battalion of *Zapadores* (Sappers) raised in 1827 and led by engineer officers. There is practically no information before **August 31, 1840** on the uniforms of engineer officers and the battalion of *Zapadores*. The regulations of that date specified: blue coat, black collar and lapels, crimson cuffs, turn-backs and piping, brass buttons; blue trousers with crimson piping; shako with crimson pompon and without cords for the men. Gray *levita* tunic-style coats. Engineer officers had gold buttons and distinctions, those attached to battalions having the crimson pompon on their shako (illustrated by G.A.Embleton in MAA 56, *The Mexican-American War 1846–48*). See the portrait on this page.

Medical Corps
The Military Medical Corps, established on November 30, 1829, gathered the existing surgeons and doctors in the army into an establishment of 85 professionals. However, their actual numbers were obviously much lower and the corps was seriously deficient; no medical staff at all were present with the army during the 1836 Texas campaign. The corps was reorganized under a colonel as director and several lieutenant-colonels as inspectors in August 1836. Military hospitals were authorized to be estab-

lished by a regulation of February 11, 1837, and ten existed by 1843. Their authorized professional staff consisted of directors, professors of departments, and practitioners of the 1st and 2nd Class – these were doctors and surgeons, the only pharmacists being at the Chihuahua hospital. The support personnel consisted of chaplains, accountants, clerks, etc.

In 1843, 48 professionals and 34 support staff were listed. There were three classes of hospitals. The 1st Class (staffs of ten to 18) were at Vera Cruz, Tampico, San Luis Potosi, Chihuahua and Matamoros. There were smaller 2nd Class hospitals (staff of five) at Tabasco, Perote and Acapulco; and Provisional 2nd Class hospitals at Jalapa and Guadalajara. The establishment was officially raised to 73 professionals on February 25, 1843, and again to 160 on January 2, 1846; but one suspects the actual numbers of the *Cuerpo Medico Militar* would have been far below the official establishment. To transport the wounded, ambulance enlisted men were also supposed to be attached to the corps from each regiment: four men per 100 combatants in peacetime, and eight in wartime.

In **August 1836** the medical officers were assigned a blue coat with green velvet collar, crimson cuffs, piping and turn-backs; a blue or white waistcoat; gold buttons, gold embroidery on the collar, gold Aesculapius badges on the turn-backs, and a plain bicorn. On **February 25, 1843** the uniform changed to a blue coat with sky-blue collar and cuffs, white piping and crimson turn-backs, gold buttons, and a medical badge on the collar; blue or white trousers; a bicorn hat laced with gold for senior officers and black velvet for subalterns; and a sword, with gold knot for senior officers and crimson-red for subalterns. The rank distinctions consisted of an elaborate system of gold laces edging the collar and cuffs, which never saw the light of day as they were cancelled six weeks later on March 23.

In **May 1846** the uniform was simplified to a blue uniform edged with crimson piping, plain gold buttons, bicorn hats, and straight sword with gold knot and black scabbard. Rank distinctions were peculiar to the corps. For instance, surgeons (*medico-cirjuanos*) had a hat with a tricolor plume; a gold embroidered buttonhole at each side of the collar, and a gold lace border at the collar and cuffs. Assistant-surgeons and garrison staff surgeons (*ayudante do cirujanos, cirujanos de las plazas*) had no plume and a gold lace at each side of the collar. When mounted, surgeons and assistant-surgeons had blue housings edged with gold and blue lace respectively. On campaign, a blue tunic-style coat piped crimson was worn. Ambulance men had a white canvas frock coat which they wore with their regimental trousers and forage caps (illustrated by G.A.Embleton in MAA 56, *The Mexican-American War 1846–48*).

*   *   *

Corps of Marines

The small Mexican Navy had a Corps of Marines, elements of which were detached in the main

Sapper Battalion sleeve badge, 1840s, showing a bursting bomb over a trophy of tools and weapons. This remarkable item, once yellow on blue though now much faded, was 'cut from the coat of a dead Mexican on the battlefield of Buena Vista by Maj. J.C.Partridge, P[ay] Master U.S. Army about three months subsequent to the battle of 22nd July 1847.' (Mr & Mrs Don Troiani Collection)

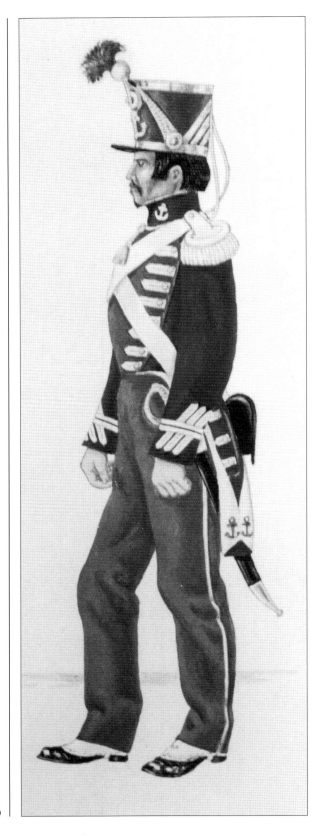

seaports. In 1824 this consisted of seven infantry companies and one company of artillery. By order of **March 22, 1837**, the Marine Infantry and Artillery were to have similar uniforms to their army counterparts except for an anchor stamped on the buttons and displayed on the collar for the Marine Infantry, an anchor across the flaming bomb for the Marine Artillery. This merely confirmed existing practice, as the 1825–26 clothing was the same as for the army except for shako plates. The infantry was assigned its own distinctive and colorful uniform by Santa Anna on **November 19, 1842** (see this page). Marines were part of the garrison of Vera Cruz, where Lt Sebastian Holzinguer heroically saved the Mexican flag during a bombardment on March 23, 1847. A company of marines was part of the Mazatlan garrison when it was taken by the US Navy on November 10–11, 1847.

Corps of Invalids

An establishment of *Invalidos* or veteran old soldiers, equal to light garrison duties, existed in Mexico since 1773. On September 11, 1829, they were organized into a four-company battalion; this served mostly in Mexico City, which it helped to defend in 1847 before withdrawing to Queretaro. There was also an invalid company at Puebla and at Tampico. The uniform at the time of independence was blue faced with sky-blue and, from 1839, was a blue coat with sky-blue collar, cuffs, lapels and turn-backs, scarlet piping, and 'Invalidos' on the collar.

The Military College

The Military College was approved in 1823 but took a few years to set up. Initially at the fortress of Perote, then in a former convent, it was transferred to Chapultepec Castle in 1841. It had only 31 cadets in 1831, and 46 when the Americans attacked the castle on September 13, 1847. The boys put up an outstanding defense; six were

Private, Marine Infantry, full dress, 1842–48. Crimson shako with brass plate and chin scales and yellow furniture, green and yellow pompon. Dark green coat, collar and cuffs, crimson lapels and piping; yellow lace and epaulettes, brass buttons; yellow anchor badge at collar, white turn-backs with crimson anchor badges; crimson trousers with yellow stripe. The slanting yellow cuff laces, pointed at both ends, denote an elite marine analogous to an infantry grenadier. Reconstruction by J.Hefter. (Anne S.K.Brown Military Collection, Providence; author's photo)

Posthumous portrait of Cadet Francisco Marquez, Military College, 1840s. Cadet Marquez was killed on September 13, 1847 in the defense of Chapultepec Castle, at the age of 15 years. He is portrayed wearing dress uniform: a blue coat with scarlet collar and cuffs edged with gold lace, scarlet piping on the turn-backs and down the front, gilt buttons and white trousers. (Museo Nacional de Historia, Mexico; author's photo)

killed, including Cadet Juan Escutia, who leapt from the highest wall wrapped in the college's flag rather than surrender. Three were wounded and the others captured; their heroism and sacrifice inspired the nation, and their memory has since been cherished.

The uniform appears to have been, from the outset, similar to that of the infantry. This was formally decreed on **November 18, 1833**, with buttons stamped *Colegio Militar*; each year the cadets were issued a coat, jacket, two pairs of trousers of fine cloth, a *cachucha* (probably a forage cap) and a shako, and a greatcoat every three years. They also received white linen trousers, black silk stocks, shirts, shoes and other necessaries. In **August 1840**, the blue coat's collar and cuffs were changed to sky-blue. The undress jacket was the same colors as the coat, and worn with a blue forage cap with scarlet piping and yellow lace. For uniforms from 1843, see Plate H3.

CIVIC MILITIA & NATIONAL GUARDS

Independent Mexico inherited a fairly elaborate militia organization from the Spanish in 1821. The urban and other more sedentary militias were organized as the *Milicia Civica* on August 8, 1822. Companies were to have 70 to 100 men, and battalions from four to six companies. Cavalry were to have 60 troopers including two trumpeters, led by a captain, a lieutenant and a sub-lieutenant. On May 5, 1823, the *Milicia Nacional de Artilleria* – the National Militia Artillery – was organized, companies numbering from 40 men including a drummer and a fifer, led by a captain, a lieutenant and a sub-lieutenant. Militiamen were to be between 16 and 50 years of age. When called up, their duties were to provide police-type services such as apprehending bandits, guarding public buildings and escorting prisoners. The units bore their state names except for Mexico City, which had *Distrito Federal* – Federal District.

In December 1827 the Civic Militia was largely devolved to the states by putting it under the control of state governors, who were responsible for its administration and its minimum enlistment quotas. In too many cases the result was that 'most of these *Civicos* are the dregs of the people, because every person who can pay 3 *reals* per month has the means to be released from service of this kind – that these soldiers have been frequently seen in liquor "on duty", subject to little discipline and always eager to loot' (PRO, FO 50/34). However, a few state governors realized that this responsibility offered an opportunity to increase their power relative to the central government. This was perhaps best understood by Governor Francisco Garcia of the state of Zacatecas, who, in the 1830s, enjoyed the support of some 17,000 men in decently organized units.

With a force to rival the federal army, Garcia was thus a powerful player whom no president could ignore – until 1835, when the Zacatecas militia was ordered dissolved.

On April 16, 1833, Mexico City's Federal District militia was reorganized into three infantry battalions, a brigade of artillery and a squadron of cavalry. On November 14 that year one infantry battalion was named *Batallon del Comercio de la Ciudad Federal* – Commerce Battalion of the Federal City – reviving the traditions of the elite 18th century Commerce Militia Regiment, in which the leaders of the business class had served. In Mexico City the Civic Militia was often the power base of opponents to the federal regime; whether for or against the current government, it was a potent political instrument whose officers were sometimes amongst the richest citizens in the nation. Eventually, by the late 1830s and early 1840s, senior generals and the conservatives in the government favored abolishing the Civic Militia and promoting a larger federal army. In 1845, President de Herrera ordered the dissolution of the Civic Militia and its replacement by a National Guard made up of volunteers.

The regulations of **August 1822** organizing the Civic Militia specified a sky-blue coat with yellow collar, cuffs and piping, sky-blue turn-backs and pantaloons. Cavalry and infantry had the same dress except that infantry units had brass buttons and cavalry white metal. The coat color was changed to blue on **May 3, 1823**. In the years that followed it appears that some militiamen preferred to wear the uniforms of the regular army and, on **January 18, 1830**, a regulation mentioned that the Civic Militia would use the same facing colors as the Permanent troops – which implied blue coats with scarlet collar and cuffs for the infantry, and red coats with green collars and cuffs for the Civic Militia cavalry. This was confirmed by the regulation of **February 16, 1833** for the Civic Militia of Mexico City, which specified a uniform similar to regular troops, with the letters 'DF' for *Distrito Federal* on the collar. In **1834**, the regulation concerning the Civic Militia of the State of Coahuila and Texas mentioned a blue coat with scarlet collar and cuffs (or yellow if scarlet was not available), brass buttons, blue trousers, and 'leather hat or helmet.' By the regulations of **May 5, 1823**, the National Militia Artillery had the same uniform as the infantry except for a gold grenade on each side of the collar, and scarlet turn-backs. The gunners' collars and cuffs were scarlet from January 1830.

One should bear in mind that Civic Militia uniforms were not compulsory, but procured if the unit or individuals could or would buy them. Those who did acquire uniforms were considered to have

Infantry officer, 1840s; this may be a National Guard uniform. Black shako with gold furniture and scarlet pompon. Blue French-style frock coat with yellow cuffs and lapels; scarlet three-point front patches and gold badges on blue collar; scarlet piping edging cuffs, lapels and down front; gold buttons and epaulettes; scarlet trousers with gold piping. (Anne S.K.Brown Military Collection, Providence; author's photo)

Infantry drum carried by the Army of the Three Guarantees, 1821. The case is painted red, but the hoops are missing. The cartouche, in natural colors, shows the Mexican eagle perched on its cactus against a landscape and sky; it is edged at the top with green, white and red ribbon (reading inwards), and at the bottom with dissimilar gold wreaths. The white banner or scroll is shadowed in blue/gray but bears no inscription. As drum cases were usually painted in the color of the drummers' coats, this may indicate that Mexican drummers had red coats from an early date. (Museo Nacional de Historia, Mexico)

performed 'a laudable and patriotic deed.' On the other hand, Civicos were to 'wear their uniforms on duty,' something that must have been interpreted according to practical considerations. For instance, Civic Militia 'irregular' cavalry in large cities may well have worn the cumbersome crested helmets, but in the countryside the typical *vaquero* saddlery and dress with broad-brimmed felt hat was certainly predominant (illustrated by G.A.Embleton in MAA 56, *The Mexican-American War 1846–48*).

National Guards

Although the Civic Militia was supposed to be the national reserve, Mexico did not have a distinct, well equipped and disciplined national volunteer force such as France's National Guards. In some states and large cities a core of citizens interested in military (and often also political) affairs kept up well equipped volunteer units. From the early 1840s there were increasing suggestions for the formation of a national reserve organization, but the government was cautious about authorizing what might become a nationwide politico-military force. The American annexation of Texas in 1845 changed the government's mind: war with the United States was becoming a distinct possibility, and a National Guard was created.

These unpaid volunteers were to be armed and clothed at their own expense and called out on active service only in case of war. The conditions demanded for joining were hard for most volunteers to meet and, outside the several uniformed units in Mexico City, the other National Guards units formed from the former militia were often poorly armed and clothed. They were under the authority of their state governments which, in effect, had to finance and administer them, but they could be called up for service by the federal government.

In 1846 the garrison of Vera Cruz included the city's National Guard battalion of 800 men, 500 men of the Orizava National Guard, 80 gunners of the National Guard Artillery company, and some 109 varied volunteers. They fought the Americans in March 1847 until the port's surrender on the 29th of the month. George C.Furber described a well ordered and well equipped garrison emerging 'battalion after battalion' from the gates of the city, appearing soldier-like 'with shouldered muskets and free step, while the rays of the sun glanced upon their bright arms… Some of the regiments were clothed in brilliant uniforms of green, trimmed with red; others in blue, trimmed also with red; others in light dress, nearly white, with red pompons… First came the columns of regulars; then followed the National Guard.'[10]

10 George C.Furber, *The Twelve Month Volunteer* (Cincinnati, 1857), pp.557–559. There is no direct evidence, but the white or off-white linen uniforms would be the most likely for the National Guard in this tropical city. The garrison also included the 2nd and 4th Line Inf and a 41-man detachment from the 11th; a piquet of the 3rd Light Inf; the Puebla, Jamiltepec & Oaxaca Activo bns, and a 60-man det from the Tehuantepec bn; 600 gunners and 80 sailors, in all c4,390 men. To these were later added green-clad lancers and marines – see Miguel Lerdo de Tejeda, *Apuntes Historicos de la Heroica Ciudad de Veracruz* (Mexico, 1857). The green uniforms trimmed with red may have been worn by marines; 2nd & 8th Line and the Activo bns probably wore blue coats trimmed with red.

In Mexico City, the Hidalgo, Bravo, Independencia, Union and Victoria National Guard battalions were organized among the skilled artisan and middle classes. They were nicknamed the 'Polkos', as it was said that their men enjoyed dancing polkas. Concerned with defending Mexico City, they mutinied on February 28, 1847, rather than go to reinforce the Vera Cruz garrison; Santa Anna had to send a large force including his Guard Hussars to restore order. By May 1847, the Americans were nearing Mexico City from the coast and from the north. The city's National Guard battalions formed Gen Pedro Anaya's 5th Brigade posted at the area of the convent of San Mateo in Churubusco. In August the battalions put up a tremendous defense of the convent, but the Americans finally prevailed due to superior firepower – the Independencia and Bravo battalions were destroyed, while the mauled Victoria was the last to withdraw. Nevertheless, some 600 men from the Mina, Union, and Patria battalions, as well as the National Guard battalions from Queretaro and Toluca, formed part of the troops defending part of the area near Chapultepec Castle in September, while the Hidalgo Battalion fought on the Tacubayba road. (See Plate H1.)

Flags and standards

The first flag of Mexico was proclaimed by Gen Augustin de Iturbide in February 1821 as the color of the Army of the Three Guarantees. It consisted of a square tricolor: green for revolution, white for religion, and red for the unity of all groups in Mexico to create the new nation. This tricolor was diagonally arranged (with the imperial crown in gold at the center added later), with the motto RELIGION, INDEPENENCIA, UNION, and at the bottom the designation of the unit. A six-point star of contrasting color was placed on each strip (see page 58). There were many variations on this pattern in the months that followed.

On November 2, 1821, the first national flag was proclaimed. It consisted of a French-style tricolor with green, white and red vertical stripes, charged with a crowned eagle (without the snake in its beak) on a cactus plant surrounded by water. On April 14, 1823, upon the fall of the Empire and the proclamation of the Republic, the crown was removed; the snake was added, as well as a wreath below the cactus plant. There have been many variations on individual flags but, on the whole, this national flag remained essentially the same until 1968, when the present design was adopted, with the eagle shown more in profile.

The tricolor national flag was the basis for the unit colors and standards. Regimental designations were added above and below the eagle at the center. The Civic Militia regulation of August 8, 1822, mentioned having the name of the province in gold letters above the

OPPOSITE **Rear view of the bugle-major's coat. Note the false horizontal pockets; the silver embroidered eagles at the junctions of the black velvet turn-backs; and the 'scissors' of silver lace in the small of the waist. (Courtesy James L.Kochan, Harper's Ferry, W.Virginia)**

eagle and the name of the town or state and the battalion number below it. This was carried on from 1845 by the National Guard, who placed the words *Guardia Nacional* above the eagle.

The San Patricio Legion had, however, a totally different color which echoed the Irish origin of its soldiers. It was described by Sam Chamberlain as a 'beautiful green silk banner…; on it glittered a silver cross and a golden harp, embroidered by the hands of the fair nuns of San Luis Potosi.'

BATTLES AND UNITS

Tampico, September 10, 1829: 2nd, 3rd, 5th, 9th & 11th Line Infantry; Tres Villas Active Militia infantry; Vera Cruz Civic Militia detachment. 12th Line Cavalry; Jalapa, Orizaba & Cordoba Line squadrons; Vera Cruz Act Mil sqn; artillery.

The Alamo (Texas), February 23–March 6, 1836: Aldama, Guadalajara, Guerrero, Jiminez, Matamoros & Morelos Line Inf; Guajanuato, 1st Mexico, Queretaro, San Luis Potosi, 1st Toluca, Tres Villas & Yucatan Act Mil inf. Santa Anna's cav escort sqn; Cuautla, Dolores, Tampico & small det from Vera Cruz & Cohula Line Cav; Rio Grande Presidial cav company; San Luis Potosi & Bajio auxiliary cav troops; Sapper Bn; artillery.

San Jacinto (Texas), April 21, 1836: Aldama, Guadalajara, Matamoros & Guerrero Line Inf; 1st Toluca Act Mil inf; Grenadier Bn & Cazadores Bn (flank cos gathered in separate temporary unit); Santa Anna's cav escort sqn; artillery.

San Antonio de Bejar (Texas), August 1842: 'Santa Anna' Bn (temporary dets from Light Inf Bn, 1st, 11th & 12th Line Inf); 'Santa Anna' Cav Regt (temporary dets from 1st, 3rd & 7th Line Cav); seven Presidial Cav cos; artillery; Indian scouts.

Palo Alto/Resaca de la Palma, May 8–9, 1846: 2nd Light Inf; 1st, 4th, 6th & 10th Line Inf; Tampico Veteran Co; Puebla Act Mil inf & Tampico Coast Guard inf; Villas del Norte auxil inf. 1st, 7th & 8th Line Cav; Light Cav of Mexico sqn; Presidial cav co; sappers; artillery.

Monterey, August 24, 1846: 2nd, 3rd & 4th Light Inf; 1st, 3rd, 4th, 6th (det), 7th & 8th (det) Line Inf; Activo de Mexico inf; Morelia, San Luis Potosi, Queretaro, Aguascaliente Act Mil inf; Monterey auxil bn. 1st, 3rd, 7th & 8th Line Cav; Jalisco Lancers; Guanatajo & San Luis Potosi Act Mil cav; Presidial cav dets; sappers; artillery.

Mesa/San Gabriel (California), January 8–9, 1847: A few Presidials; California Mil cav & artillery.

Buena Vista/Angostura, February 22–23, 1847: 1st, 2nd, 3rd & 4th Light Inf; 1st, 3rd, 4th & 11th Line Inf; Fijo de Mexico inf; 1st & 3rd Activo de Mexico inf; Puebla

& Tampico Coast Guard Act Mil inf (dets); Leon Nat Guard inf. Hussars of Supreme Powers; 1st, 3rd, 5th, 7th & 8th Line Cav; Light Cav of Mexico; Puebla Light Cav sqn; Tulancingo Cuirassiers; Cazadores a Caballo; Guanajuato, San Luis, Michoacan & Oaxaca Act Mil cav regts; sappers; artillery.

Vera Cruz, March 9–29, 1847: 3rd Light Inf (det); 2nd, 8th & 11th (det) Line Inf; Puebla, Tampico, Jamiltepec, Oaxaca, Tehuantepec (det), Tuxpan (co) & Alvarado (co) Act Mil bns; Vera Cruz, Orizava & Oaxaca Nat Guard inf; Nat Guard cav; artillery; Marine artillery co; Vera Cruz Nat Guard artillery; Sapper Bn (co).

Cerro Gordo, April 18, 1847: Guard Grens; 1st, 2nd & 3rd Light Inf; 3rd, 4th, 6th & 11th Line Inf; Puebla Act Mil inf; Libertad Nat Guard inf. Hussars of Supreme Powers; 5th & 9th Line Cav; Light Cav of Mexico; Puebla Light Cav sqn; Tulancingo Cuirassiers; Oaxaca Act Mil cav; Army & Marine artillery.

Padierna, August 19–20, 1847: 1st, 10th & 12th Line Inf; Tampico Coast Guard inf. 2nd, 3rd, 7th & 8th Line Cav; Guanajuato Act Mil cav; Puebla Light Cav sqn; artillery.

Churubusco, August 19–20, 1847: 1st, 2nd & 4th Light Inf; 11th Line Inf; San Patricio inf; Victoria, Hidalgo, Bravo & Independencia Nat Guard inf. Hussars of Supreme Powers; 9th Line Cav; Tulancingo Cuirassiers; artillery.

Molino del Rey, September 8, 1847: 1st & 2nd Light Inf; 1st, 10th & 11th Line Inf; Fijo de Mexico inf; artillery.

Mexico City valley, September 12–14, 1847: Guard Grens; 1st, 2nd & 3rd Light Inf; 11th Line Inf; Invalid Bn of Mexico; 1st Activo de Mexico inf. Hussars of Supreme Powers; 2nd, 3rd, 5th, 7th, 8th & 9th Line Cav; Tulancingo Cuirassiers; Michoacan & Oaxaca Act Mil cav; Puebla Light Cav sqn; artillery.

Chapultepec, September 13, 1847: 10th Line Inf; Fijo de Mexico inf; Colegio Militar cadets; Mina, Union, Queretaro, Toluca, Patria & San Blas Nat Guard inf; sappers; artillery.

Mazatlan, November 10–11, 1847: California Inf Bn; Marine Inf (co); Mazatlan Nat Guard inf (co). Cavalry (det); Sapper Bn (det); artillery.

The medium green collar is edged with scarlet piping. On the right side it bears the number '4°' embroidered in silver in a palm and sword pattern; on the left, a foliate 'L$^{\circ}$' for *'Ligero'*. The 4th Light Infantry received its colors in June 1846; after serving at Monterey that September and at Buena Vista in February 1847, it was wiped out at Churubusco on August 19 that year. (Courtesy James L.Kochan, Harper's Ferry, W.Virginia)

SELECT BIBLIOGRAPHY

Manuscripts
At the Anne S.K.Brown Military Collection, Brown University, Providence, RI (USA): Detmar Finke notes; F.P.Todd Albums; J.Hefter notes and plates. At the Public Records Office (PRO), Kew (UK): Foreign Office (FO) class 50 (Mexico), volumes for 1823–1827, 1835–1838, 1846–1847 and FO 97 for 1824–1825. At the Archivo Nacional de la Nacion (Mexico City): Primer Imperio, Hacienda for 1822–1823.

Books and articles
Bauer, Jack L., *The Mexican War 1846–1848* (New York, 1974)

Collecion de Leyes y Decretos publicado en el año de 1839 (Mexico, 1852)

Collecion de Ordones y Decretos…de la Nacion Mexicana (Mexico, 1829)

Castaneda, Carlos E., *The Mexican Side of the Texan Revolution* (Austin, 1970). Essential source on this topic.

Castillo Negrete, Emilio del, *Historia Militar del Mexico en el Siglo XIX* (Mexico, 1883)

Cotner, Thomas Ewing, *The Military and Political Career of José Joaquin De Herrera 1792–1854* (Austin, 1954)

DePalo, William A., *The Mexican National Army 1822–1852* (College Station, TX, 1997). Superlative academic work on the army's politics, organization and campaigns, but not on its material culture.

Duclas, Robert, *La vie quotidienne au Mexique au milieu du XIXe siècle* (Paris, 1993)

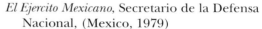

The lower sleeve and cuff, showing the medium green cuff flap edged with scarlet piping set on the black velvet cuff, and one of the four sets of silver lace chevrons. Note the rounded front edge of the cuff flap, similar to that in the Santa Anna portrait on page 3. Originally each chevron had one tassel at the center and one at each end. (Courtesy James L.Kochan, Harper's Ferry, W.Virginia)

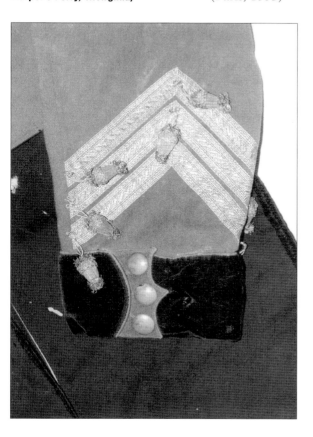

El Ejercito Mexicano, Secretario de la Defensa Nacional, (Mexico, 1979)

Field, Ron, *The Mexican War 1846–1848* (London, 1997)

Haythornthwaite, Philip, ill. Paul Hannon, *The Alamo and the Texan War of Independence 1833–36* (Osprey MAA 173: London, 1986)

Hefter, Joseph, with Anne S.K.Brown & A. Nieto, *El Soldado Mexicano – The Mexican Soldier 1837–1847* (Mexico, 1958). This bilingual booklet is a pioneering work and remains an essential study on army organization and uniforms.

Hefter, Joseph, 'Cronica del Traje Militar en Mexico del Siglo XVI al XX', *Artes de Mexico*, No. 102, año XV (1968)

Katcher, Philip, ill. G.A.Embleton, *The Mexican-American War 1846–48* (Osprey MAA 56: London, 1976)

Legislacion mexicana, compiled by Manuel Dublan and José Maria Lozano, (Mexico, 1876–1912), 42 volumes. The appendix to Vol.1 is an especially important source.

Linati, Claude, *Costumes civils, militaires et religieux du Mexique* (Brussels, c1827)

Nevin, David, *The Mexican War* (Alexandria, VA, 1978). Good illustrations.

Design of the colors for infantry regiments of the Army of the Three Guarantees, used February to November 1821. White star on red stripe, red star on green stripe, green star on white stripe; white cartouche, black lettering, gold and red crown and ornaments. (Anne S.K.Brown Military Collection, Providence; author's photo)

This color of the Mina National Guard Artillery is typical of Mexican Army colors from 1824. This example was saved from capture at Molino del Rey (at the cost of his life) by a sub-lieutenant who tore it from its staff and wrapped it round his body. The green/ white/ red tricolor bears the eagle in shades of gold, between lines of black lettering; the ribbon bow at top left is red with a gold fringe. (Museo Nacional de Historia, Mexico; author's photo)

Niles, John M., and L.T. Pease, *History of South America and Mexico... to which is annexed... a detailed account of the Texian Revolution and War* (Hartford, 1838), Vol.1

Memoria del secretario de estado y del despacho de Guerra y marina, leída a las cámaras del Congresso nacional de la República Mexicana [title varies]. Annual reports published in Mexico City from the Minister of War and Marine to the Mexican National Congress. The 1840s volumes include uniform and arms issues.

The Papers of the Texas Revolution 1835–1836, edited by John H.Jenkins, (Austin, 1973), 9 volumes

Penot, Jacques, *Les relations entre la France et le Mexique de 1808 et 1840* (PhD thesis, University of Paris X, February 23, 1976)

Plana Mayor del Ejercito, *Noticia Historica de los Cuerpos de Infanteria y Caballeria del Ejercito Mexicano* (Mexico, 1851). Essential source.

'Regulations for the Civic Militia of Coahuila and Texas, 1834', Richard G.Santos ed., *Texas Military History*, IV, Winter 1967

Salas, Elizabeth, *Soldaderas in the Mexican Military: Myth and History* (Austin, 1990)

Zoraida Vasquez, Josefina, *La intervencion nortamericana 1846-1848* (Mexico, 1997). A well balanced account of the Mexican view of the war and its army, finely illustrated.

THE PLATES

A: REGULAR & ACTIVE MILITIA CAVALRY

A1: Colonel, Moncada Dragoon Regiment, 1821

This figure is based on a full length portrait of Don Juan Nepomencino de Moncada y Berio, colonel of the Moncada Provincial Dragoons, painted almost certainly in 1821. The uniform was a yellow coat with black facings, scarlet piping and turn-backs, silver buttons and lace. Nepomencino is shown with silver epaulettes each bearing a gold six-pointed star; and a bicorn with wide silver lace, a black feather edging, and tricolor plumes and cockade. The Moncada Dragoons were among the units drafted to form the 2nd Permanent Cavalry Regiment from December 24, 1821. (Banco Nacional de Mexico)

A2: Officer, 9th Permanent Cavalry Regiment, c1824–33

This full dress is based on the December 6, 1824, uniform regulations which called for a scarlet coat with green collar and cuffs, scarlet piping edging the green and vice versa, white metal buttons; gray trousers for campaign service and blue trousers for garrison service, both with leather strapping; half boots, yellow cloak, and dragoon helmet. Officers had silver buttons, badges and epaulettes and, for full dress, white breeches and high boots. His helmet is based on a superb example in the Museo Nacional de Historia, and has the long black horse hair falling mane like that of French cuirassiers or dragoons, rather than the stuffed 'caterpillar' crest usually shown.

A3: Field officer, Active Militia cavalry, 1824–33

By the regulations of December 1824 the Active Militia cavalry had uniforms of the reversed colors to the Permanent cavalry: green coat, scarlet collar and cuffs, green piping edging scarlet and vice versa, with other items the same as the Permanent units. It was further specified that all officers and generals of the Active Militia cavalry would wear helmets on ordinary duty and parade. For gala and official state functions, officers and generals were required to appear in a coat with tails and a bicorn hat.

B: INFANTRY & STAFF, 1820s-1830s

B1: Fusilier of infantry, 1826

This figure is based on a watercolor by Capt B.de Valmont, a French naval officer, who painted soldiers he saw as he toured Latin America in the 1820s. His *soldat mexicain* has a blue coat with scarlet collar, cuffs, piping and turn-backs, three vertical buttons on possibly a scarlet cuff flap, and blue shoulder straps piped scarlet; white trousers and gaiters, and black shako with tricolor cockade (from the outside, white, red and green) and pointed tuft. No shako plate is shown, which probably indicates that this soldier's dress predates the 1826 issue imported from Europe. The accoutrements include the narrow leather waistbelt, a favorite of Mexican soldiers; the musket is the Spanish M1801. (Valmont Ms, Cabinet des Estampes, Bibliothèque Nationale, Paris)

B2: Aide-de-camp detached from the Horse Grenadiers Regiment, 1821–23

The entourage of senior generals often presented a glittering array of superb uniforms. This magnificently dressed ADC wears the officer's uniform worn by the Regiment of Horse Grenadiers from 1821 to 1823. Until disbanded in 1825 this was Mexico's 'Guard' cavalry regiment, and several of its officers would have acted as aides to generals. It initially wore a hussar uniform which appears to have followed French styles closely. The white dolman is trimmed with eight rows of green cords, a scarlet collar and cuffs; the green pelisse is edged with black fur and trimmed with silver cord and buttons; green trousers were trimmed with a silver stripe (obscured here) having a line of scarlet piping at the center. The uniform is completed by a black fur busby with red, white and green bag, silver cords and, most likely, a tricolor plume; a green and silver barrel sash and black sabretache. This uniform later changed to a scarlet coat with green collar, cuffs, turn-backs and piping, the sleeves trimmed with white cord, the cuffs and collar edged with white lace, and the cuffs and pocket flaps having three white laces; green pantaloons, a fur cap with white cords, and a green cloak and housings. The officers had silver lace and buttons, white pantaloons and high 'Napoleon' boots.

Engraving from the 1822 dress regulations for administrative officers, showing patterns of lace. The broad lace is for Intendants and other senior officers, the narrow for junior officers, and the eagles were displayed on the cuffs by some ranks – see Plate B3. The crown was removed and a snake added to the eagle's beak in 1823. (Archivo General de la Nacion, Mexico)

Infantry shako plate, 1830s–40s – probably a general issue item, as it has no unit designation. Mexican shako and bearskin plates were often made in France, and the designs were inspired by plates used by French National Guard units. (San Jacinto Museum of History; photo James L.Kochan)

This tradition of showy dress for ADCs went on for many years. During the 1836 Texas campaign, Col Almonte, Gen Santa Anna's ADC, wore 'a light blue coat with a green collar, red belt [sash] and silver buttons.' In 1839, Lady Calderon de La Barca noted Gen Victoria's ADCs 'in a showy uniform all covered with gold, with colossal epaulets and a towering plume of rainbow-colored feathers'; and a couple of years later she saw 'three very magnificent aides-de-camp' of Gen Valencia. (Frances Calderon de La Barca, *Life in Mexico*, London, 1843)

B3: Comisario de Guerra, undress, 1820s–1830s
The undress uniform of administrative officers was a green coat with scarlet collar, cuffs and turn-backs, an inch-wide gold lace edging the collar and cuffs, and the rank badges on the cuffs as on the dress coat – a *comisario de guerra* had two eagles on each cuff. The pantaloons were white, with black 'half boots.' Other items were the same as for the dress uniform. (Archivo General de la Nacion, Primer Imperio, Hacienda, Vol. 1871–15, folios 16–18)

C: INFANTRY & ARTILLERY, 1820s–1830s
C1: Drummer, infantry, c1830
The uniforms of drummers, buglers and trumpeters are never mentioned in orders and rarely shown. From what little evidence has been found, it would appear that they wore uniforms of reversed colors, from the earliest formation of the Mexican army. A drummer is shown in a scarlet coatee with the distinctive Mexican musician's sleeve lace and tassels at Iturbide's proclamation on May 1, 1822; paintings of the main square in Mexico City in the late 1820s and 1830s show blue-clad soldiers with drummers wearing red

coats, white trousers and black shakos. In the painting of the 1829 battle of Tampico, a red-coated soldier caring for a wounded comrade has a brass drum next to him – and it was part the drummers' duties to help the infirmary. Early drums were of wood painted red, with appropriate devices; but, seemingly from the mid-1820s, French-style brass drums apparently became predominant.

C2: Private, 3rd Permanent Infantry Regiment, c1830
This figure is based on infantry soldiers shown in the background to Santa Anna's c1830 portrait at the Museo de la Ciudad de Mexico. They wear a blue coat with scarlet collar, cuffs, piping and turn-backs, red shoulder wings of raised crescent shape, blue cuff flaps with three buttons, and brass buttons; white trousers; a black shako with yellow bands and red cords and plume, a brass plate and chin scales; and white accoutrements, including a black cartridge box on top of which is a small light gray roll. The scarlet shoulder wings and shako plume and cords might be grenadiers' distinctions, but fringed epaulettes would be more likely; also this source shows no pointed laces at the cuffs, and no hangers are carried – both typical distinctions of Mexican grenadiers.

C3: Gunner, Corps of Artillery, 1820s–1830s
Until 1840 artillery uniforms appear to have been similar to those of the infantry except for the distinctive flaming bomb badges, and to follow the dress of the Spanish Artillery worn at the time of independence. This consisted of a blue coat with scarlet collar, cuffs, turn-backs and piping, blue lapels and cuff flaps piped scarlet, yellow metal buttons, and yellow flaming bomb badges on the collar and turn-backs; a black shako with yellow metal fittings and lace and a red plume and cords; and red epaulettes (gold buttons and epaulettes for officers). Initially, only the Mexican tricolor cockade replaced the red Spanish cockade. Following the reorganization of the early 1820s the uniform was little changed apart from becoming single-breasted without lapels, as shown here. Lists of clothing for the Permanent artillery in 1825–26 included, for the foot artillery, blue coats with pairs of epaulettes, blue frocks, blue trousers and blue fatigue caps; for the mounted brigade, blue coatees with pairs of epaulettes, blue pantaloons probably strapped with leather, blue capes, blue fatigue caps, and blue housings and valises possibly edged with yellow lace. All uniforms had brass buttons and would have been trimmed with scarlet.

D: LINE INFANTRY & CAVALRY, 1830s
D1: First Sergeant, Hidalgo Infantry Regt, c1832–36
In January 1832 the government contracted for 10,000 infantry uniforms which added scarlet lapels, and white (instead of scarlet) piping to the collar, cuffs, lapels and turn-backs. This was abolished on June 13, 1833; but by that time most if not all had been made and issued. By regulation the uniforms had to last for two and half years (and probably for a great deal longer, in practice). Mexican infantry units in Texas during 1835–36 could therefore be seen wearing both types of coats: with scarlet lapels and white piping, and single-breasted with scarlet piping. The epaulettes illustrated are the badges of this rank, under the January 1830 regulations. (Notes by Joseph Hefter at the Anne S.K.Brown Military Collection, Brown University)

D2: Grenadier, summer dress, c1836–38

Infantrymen had a hot weather dress consisting of a white cotton round jacket and trousers, the jacket often having red collar and cuffs, and sometimes being illustrated with red short tail turn-backs, raised crescent wings or epaulettes. The three yellow laces pointed at both ends, shown here on the cuffs and forearms, were a traditional Spanish distinction for grenadiers. The shako cover was white. 'The dress that the Mexican infantry and artillery troops of that day wore, on the march and in action, was their fatigue suit, consisting of white cotton round jackets & trousers, with black shoulder belts crossed on the breast,' recollected R.M.Potter during the 1836 Texas campaign. Some troops had fatigue caps with this white uniform. A French naval officer, the Prince de Joinville, noted Mexican soldiers defending Vera Cruz in 1838 as wearing white uniforms with red epaulettes and white forage caps with a red band. (Prince de Joinville, 'Vieux souvenirs', *Neptunia*, No. 131, 1978)

D3: Trooper, Permanent cavalry, c1832–36

The January 1832 contract specified a scarlet cloth coat with green collar, cuffs and lapels, linen lining and white metal buttons; cloth pantaloons (overalls) with leather strapping and cloth stripes; an undress linen jacket and trousers, with a forage cap. This uniform would (officially) be replaced after two and a half years; the leather helmet, garnished with brass plate, comb and chin scales and a goat hair crest, had to last five years, as did a cape with white metal buttons, cloth housings edged with a cotton lace, and a green valise with red edging. The Mexican cavalry in the 1836 Texas campaign was recalled as follows by R.M.Potter: 'The dragoons wore short red coats, blue cloth trousers & high black leather helmets, decorated with horse hair or bearskin. They were armed with lances, sabres, carbines & holster pistols.'

E: CALIFORNIA, 1830s–1840s

E1: Trooper, Presidial cavalry, Lower California, c1839

Presidial troops had blue uniforms since the 1770s but, during the later 1830s, red coatees were sent to companies in Lower California and Chihuahua. These appear to have had green collar and cuffs and white metal buttons. Reports from Presidial companies also listed linen jackets and trousers and forage caps. New Mexico companies, and probably most others, had blue coats. Note the overalls worn unbuttoned at the lower leg; and the short *escopeta* musket, with a long brass scroll trigger guard. (*Memoria del secretario de estado... de Guerra y marina... 11 de marzo de 1845,* Mexico, 1845)

E2: Officer, Fijo de California Battalion, 1842–47

By decree of January 19, 1842, the uniform was to be blue coat with scarlet collar, cuffs and turn-backs, contrasting piping, yellow metal, and on the collar the letters 'F C'; blue pantaloons with scarlet piping, and a shako with brass furniture. The officers would have had gold epaulettes and buttons. (Plana Mayor del Ejercito, *Noticia Historica...*1851)

E3: Trooper, Militia cavalry, 1846–47

California's militia featured a few companies of 'auxiliary' artillery such as the one at San José, and regiments of militia, much of which was mounted. In 1845, as it withdrew the Fijo de California Bn, the government in Mexico City

Brass epaulette, probably from the uniform of a Mexican infantryman; the green fringe may indicate an Active Militia sergeant. Stamped brass shoulder boards became common in the 1840s; some were stamped with corps insignia – examples are a surviving pair from the Sapper (*Zapadores*) battalion, and another from the artillery. (United States Military Academy Museum, West Point; author's photo)

encouraged the reinforcement of auxiliary troops in California to resist foreign aggression and maintain internal order. In August 1846 the US Navy and Marines occupied Monterey and Los Angeles, but soon evacuated when some 400 mounted militia lancers appeared. The Americans were back in late December and, on January 9, 1847, defeated the charges of the California militia lancers in a hard fight. The militia cavalry dressed mainly in their *vaquero* style breeches covered by overalls buttoned at the side, usually a red, white and green waist sash but also plain red, and black high-crowned hats. Some wore uniform red, but more often green jackets trimmed with yellow or white piping or lace with one or, more frequently, two rows of buttons on the breast. The lance pennons were shown as red and, in this case, single-tailed. (1846 drawings by W.Myers in Harry Knill, *Early Los Angeles*, Santa Barbara, 1984)

F: CAVALRY, 1839–46

F1: Trooper, Light Cavalry, 1840–46

From August 31, 1840, the uniform of all light cavalry units was ordered to be a sky-blue coat with scarlet collar, cuffs, turn-backs and piping; blue pantaloons with a red stripe and leather strapping; a shako; sky-blue cape, and housings edged with red. By 1846 this had changed, with an issue of 379 scarlet coats.

F2: Trooper, Husares de la Guardia de los Supremos Poderes, 1843–46

Being one of Santa Anna's favorite units, the hussars were well supplied with fancy uniforms and weapons. The hussar uniform assigned from December 19, 1843 consisted of a scarlet dolman with light blue (given as *azul nevado* – 'ice blue') collar and cuffs, white cords and central lace, white metal buttons; a light blue pelisse trimmed with white cords and buttons and black fur; light blue trousers with a white stripe; a fur busby with red bag and white cords and a metal plate with the name of the unit; light blue cloth housings edged white, but a round red valise edged white. This changed to a more standard uniform during the war with the United States as, in 1846, the regiment was issued 141 scarlet coats and 567 blue coats.

F3: Trooper, cavalry uniform, c1845–48

According to sketches and descriptions mostly made by Americans, the aspect of the general issue blue uniform was as follows: blue single-breasted coat with scarlet collar, cuffs, shoulder tufts, piping and turn-backs, brass buttons; sky-blue or light blue-gray trousers with a red stripe; black French style shako with brass plate and chin scales, scarlet or tricolor plume; blue housings edged with scarlet, white accoutrements, sabers, lances with red pennants and carbines. (Samuel E.Chamberlain, *My Confessions*, New York, 1856)

G: INFANTRY, 1839–47

G1: First Sergeant, 4th Light Infantry Regiment, 1846–47

This unit, although raised only on March 30, 1846, was well appointed, as it was one of Santa Anna's favored regiments. He assigned it a uniform of blue with crimson cuffs, lapels and turn-backs; green collar, cuff flaps and piping; brass buttons, and an eagle turn-back ornament; the blue trousers had crimson piping. A surviving coat has the collar piped red with '4°' in yellow on the right side and 'L°' on the left, yellow cuff lace and small green three-pointed cuff flaps; white piping edges the turn-backs, tail pocket flaps and pleats. The buttons are plain. The red epaulettes are this NCO's badges of rank, and the three pointed gold laces above the

cuff would indicate an elite company. The shako had a green pompon and a brass bugle horn plate with the numeral '4'.

G2: Fusilier, Fijo de Mexico Battalion, 1843–47

Raised from 1843, the Permanent garrison battalion of Mexico City fought at Angostura, Padierna, Molino del Rey and Chapultepec. Its uniform was a white coat with green collar, cuffs and turn-backs, the collar with gold lace edging and the unit's initials; scarlet piping, green epaulettes and brass buttons; sky-blue trousers with scarlet stripe; shako with brass chin scales and plate bearing the national arms and unit initials; cockade; green pompon for fusiliers, red for grenadiers and white for light infantry. (*Legislacion Mexicana*, IV)

G3: Officer, Active Militia, 1842–47

The Active Militia had the same uniforms as the Permanent infantry until April 1842 when a distinct uniform was specified: blue coat with scarlet collar, cuffs, lapels and turn-backs; yellow piping; brass buttons stamped with unit number and name; sky-blue trousers with scarlet piping; garnished shako with a scarlet pompon. The officers had gold buttons and epaulettes; note the shako with gold lace and plate and tricolor cockade. Our figure is based on a miniature of an officer who has narrow yellow twist cord as false buttonholes to embellish the standard uniform, and a shako with a tricolor pompon rather than scarlet. (Museo Nacional de Historia)

H: DEFENCE OF MEXICO CITY, 1847

H1: Fusilier, Bravos National Guard Battalion, 1845–47

The battalions raised in Mexico City and its suburbs from 1845 had good uniforms patterned after French infantry dress regulations issued that year. These featured the somewhat tapered shako; the blue *levita* tunic-style coat with three-quarter length skirt all around; and bright red trousers. The battalions seemingly all had the same uniform and were distinguished only by the battalion name on the brass oval shako plate. James Walker traveled with the American army and his painting of the San Mateo convent at Churubusco on August 20, 1847, shows the Mexican defenders – wounded, dead or prisoners – in the French-style blue tunics with

Officer's gorget, c1820s–40s: gilt with silver badge of Mexican eagle, with the 'Liberty cap' on the rays above. Judging from the badge, this is a Mexican-made gorget; more elaborate examples were imported from France. (San Jacinto Museum of History; photo James L.Kochan)

Officer's gilt sword belt buckles. From the styles, the round clasp is probably French-made, the rectangular plate of local manufacture. (San Jacinto Museum of History; photo James L.Kochan)

scarlet collars and cuffs, or white undress jackets with scarlet collars and cuffs; scarlet epaulettes or shoulder boards; blue forage caps with scarlet turn-up and tassels; shakos with brass plates and scarlet pompons; white crossbelts and, most notably, bright red trousers. These Mexican troops were most certainly members of the Bravos and Hidalgos National Guard battalions of Mexico City, who, with the San Patricio Legion and some artillery, put up a ferocious fight at the convent. (Shako of Bravos National Guard Bn in Connecticut Historical Society, Hartford)

H2: Officer, San Blas Active Militia Coast Guard Battalion, 1847

On active duty since 1825, this unit was converted into the 3rd Permanent Infantry Regiment in June 1846, and was destroyed at Cerro Gordo in April 1847. On July 1, 1847, the San Blas battalion was revived and quickly re-raised, joining Gen Rangel's Brigade defending Mexico City. Its light infantry company prevented the establishment of an American battery on September 12. The next day three of its companies – about 400 officers and men – defended the hill to Chapultepec Castle against an overwhelming American force, stubbornly fighting to the last. Commander Felipe de Santiago Xicotencatl died from multiple wounds, wrapped in the battalion's colors; only one officer and a few men, all wounded, escaped, all the others being killed, wounded or taken prisoner in this heroic stand. The battalion's appearance on that day is largely unknown, but it probably had the shako or forage cap, the blue *levita* illustrated or a gray frock coat, and sky-blue or white trousers. (Miguel A.Sanchez Lamego, *El Batallon de San Blas 1825–1855*, Mexico, 1964)

H3: Cadet, Military College, service dress, 1847

From December 8, 1843, the cadets were assigned a dress uniform consisting of a blue single-breasted coat with crimson cuffs, collar, piping and turn-backs, gilt buttons bearing *Colegio Militar*, and gold lace edging the collar and cuffs; blue trousers (white in summer), white gloves, and black cloth stock. Headgear was a black shako with crimson top band and plume and brass flaming bomb plate and chin scales, silk and woolen cords. The college's four drummers

and two buglers had green coats and green shako plumes. For ordinary dress, the cadets had a blue *levita* tunic-style coat with red collar and cuffs and a blue peaked cap worn with blue or white trousers. The service dress was the one worn by the adolescent cadets during their heroic defense of Chapultepec Castle on September 13, 1847. This consisted of a light gray frock coat with a red three-pointed patch on each side of the collar front, and red-striped gray trousers; a French-style blue forage cap was piped red, with yellow lace edging the turn-up and a yellow tassel.[11] Accoutrements were black with square brass plates, and the cadets had cut-down muskets. (Posthumous portrait of Cadet Augustin Melgar, 1829–47, reproduced in Hefter, 'Cronica del Traje Militar...'; *Memoria del Ministerio... de guerra y marina...*, 1846; portraits of cadets at the Museo Nacional de Historia, Mexico City)

---

11 There are detail variations, e.g. red cuff flaps, gray forage caps, Baker rifles, and crimson trousers for bandsmen, but these are inconclusive as they do not appear in contemporary documentation or artwork.

INDEX